RAIL CENTRES:
WOLVERHAMPTON

RAIL CENTRES:
WOLVERHAMPTON

PAUL COLLINS

Nottingham

Booklaw Publications

Previous page, left:
The B&W Wombourn line closed officially on 1 March 1965. This view of 43XX No 9318 working a Crewe bound goods into Wombourn station on 3 September 1954 recalls busier times on the line. *Donald Kelk*

Previous page, right
Class 90 electric locomotive No 90025 approaches Wolverhampton from Oxley carriage sidings with ecs (including a Mk 3 Driving Van Trailer) on 9 September 1989.
Brian Morrison

First published 1990 by Ian Allan Ltd

©P. Collins 1990

This edition published 2008 by Booklaw Publications 382, Carlton Hill, Nottingham NG4 1JA

ISBN 1-901945-23-5

Printed by The Amadeus Press, Cleckheaton, West Yorkshire

Contents

'Midline'-liveried Class 310/1 EMU No 310104 runs along the Birmingham canal near Dudley Port with the 10.22 Stoke-on-Trent to Walsall via Wolverhampton service on 9 September 1989.
Brian Morrison

Acknowledgements

Almost 10 years ago my fledgling interest in railways was first nurtured by attending the long-running series of WEA Railway History courses tutored by Michael Hale in Stourbridge each year. Michael was also responsible for first bringing to my attention the intricate historical tangle surrounding the development of the railways in my place of birth: Wolverhampton. Before going on to name those who have assisted me with my research for this book I would like to place on record this writer's gratitude for the diligent work of the late C. R. Clinker, whose name, as author, compiler and reviser, I continually came across.

I am grateful to the following individuals; organisations; societies and journals without whose help this book would not have been so complete, or so enjoyable to write: Apple (UK) Ltd; John Bates; Birmingham Reference Library and Local Studies Department; Branch Line Society; British Rail Staff at Wolverhampton Station, Oxley Carriage Sidings, Wednesfield Road Goods, Wolverhampton and Brierley Hill Steel Terminals; Broad Gauge Society; Celtip Computers Ltd; Tom Cockeram; June Collins; county record offices at Shrewsbury and Stafford; Ray Cresswell and Brierley Office Products Ltd; Dunns Photographic Services Ltd; Keith Gale; Ted Hanson, and all those working on the restoration of Low Level station; Mellanie Hartland; Historical Model Railway Society; Keith Hodgkins; John Horsley-Denton; Ironbridge Gorge Museum; Ironbridge Institute; Staff at the Libraries in Brierley Hill, Dudley, Langley Green, Stourbridge, Walsall; Michael Mensing; *Modern Railways;* Neil Pitts; John Powell; *Railway Gazette; Railway Magazine; Railway Observer; Railway World;* Liz Rees and Jonathan Everall of Wolverhampton Archives; Patrick Thorn; *Trains Illustrated;* University of Aston; University of Birmingham; Mike Waller; John Wilbur and the Staff at the Public Affairs Department, British Rail, Midland Region in Birmingham; Ned Williams; Amanda Winkworth; Wolverhampton Metropolitan Borough Council Technical Services Department.

Paul Collins
Wollaston, Stourbridge, West Midlands

Abbreviations

ABC	Automatic Buffing Coupler	LSWR	London & South Western Railway
B&L	Birmingham & Liverpool Railroad	MSC	Manpower Services Commission
B&O	Birmingham & Oxford Junction Railway	MSLR	Manchester Sheffield & Lincolnshire Railway
BR	British Railways	MBW&MJR	Midland Birmingham Wolverhampton & Milford Junction Railway
BRB	British Railways Board		
BRUTE	British Rail's Universal Trolley Equipment	MGR	merry-go-round
		NA&H	Newport Abergavenny & Hereford Railway
BTC	British Transport Commission		
B&W	Bridgnorth & Wolverhampton Railway	NSR	North Staffordshire Railway
BW&D	Birmingham Wolverhampton & Dudley Railway	O&R	Oxford & Rugby Railway
		OWW	Oxford Worcester & Wolverhampton Railway
DGMO	District Goods Manager's Office		
DMU	diesel multiple-unit	PCD	parcels concentration depot
ecs	empty coaching stock	S&B	Shrewsbury & Birmingham Railway
EMU	electric multiple-unit	S&C	Shrewsbury & Chester Railway
GCR	Great Central Railway	SECR	South Eastern & Chatham Railway
GJR	Grand Junction Railway	WM	West Midland Railway
GWR	Great Western Railway	WMPTE	West Midlands Passenger Transport Executive
HST	High Speed Train		
L&Y	Lancashire & Yorkshire Railway	WR	Western Region
L&B	London & Birmingham Railway	W&WR	Wolverhampton & Walsall Railway
LMR	London Midland Region	WW&MJ	Wolverhampton Walsall & Midland Junction Railway
LMS	London Midland & Scottish Railway		
LNWR	London & North Western Railway		

Introduction

Wolverhampton is 122 miles northwest of London, 14 miles northwest of Birmingham and 16 miles south of Stafford. With a population now in excess of 260,000 it ranks as one of the largest towns in the country. Its prosperity has always been closely allied with that of the neighbouring Black Country and Birmingham conurbations, but Wolverhampton can also lay claim to a number of events and citizens that give it an importance in its own right.

Notable events occurring in Wolverhampton include the building of the country's first Government School of Practical Art in 1854 and a world record seven-mile manned balloon ascent in September 1862. Following Prince Albert's death, Queen Victoria made her first public appearance there in November 1866 and in April 1900 it was one of the last places she was seen in public. In 1902 the town staged a six-month Art & Industrial Exhibition, the largest of its kind in the country since 1851 and Wolverhampton was also the first town in the country to install modern traffic lights, on 11 February 1928.

Notable people with Wolverhampton associations include: Sir William Congreve, the engineer; Edward Bird (1772-1819), the artist; Sarah Siddons (1755-1831), the actress; her brother, the actor John Kemble (1757-1823), and Dame Maggie Teyte (1888-1976), the singer. The town's citizens also became involved in historic events and achievements. The Hon C. P. Villiers was a Wolverhampton MP for 63 years, a record unsurpassed today. Moses Ironmonger, twice Mayor, received the first telephone call made in public, from his friend Alexander Graham Bell. Button Gwinnett, an ex-Wolverhampton tea merchant, became Georgia's first governor, and the second person to sign the Declaration of Independence. America was also the destination of Wolverhampton's acknowledged actor and painter Edwin Booth, whose son, one John Wilkes Booth, who assassinated President Lincoln in Washington in 1865.

In more recent times, after World War 2, Wolverhampton became the focus of attention for social researchers, including Sheldon's pioneering study of elderly people's problems, and the social and industrial survey which accredited the town the status of 'Midland City'; both published in 1948. Cinema and television cameras often came to the town also, to conduct vox pop street interviews; probably the best known being on the wearing of mini skirts, which contained the reply: 'I can't see anyone wear-ring anythinng like that mee-self – at least norrin Wulva'amptun.'

Wolverhampton's railway connections began early, as in nearby Oxley Hall was born one William Huskisson. As both President of the Board of Trade, and an MP for Liverpool, he was present at the opening of the Liverpool & Manchester Railway on 15 September 1830. Momentarily distracted, he became caught between the Duke of Wellington's carriage and the locomotive *Rocket,* passing on the other line; sustaining injuries from which he later died, becoming the first person in history to be killed as the result of a railway accident.

1: Wolverhampton — Its Character and Development

The settlement of Wolverhampton was established in 985 when King Æthelred granted lands there to a Lady Wulfrun. Henry II granted a charter to hold a market in 1258 and the town prospered from the wool trade until the 16th century, when its trade declined with the growth of woollen cloth production in Yorkshire.

Wolverhampton's Industrial Development

Iron had been smelted, and coal found, in the Wolverhampton area as early as 1272. The Civil War boosted demand for iron, as it did for secrecy, something which the town's craftsmen lockmakers quickly responded to. Both trades flourished, and by 1750 the town's oldest surviving detailed map shows 1,440 dwellings there, home to 7,454 people. About then a new trade entered the town; the manufacture of tinplate and japanned wares: iron, tin or papier mâché tea trays, tea caddies etc, sealed in lacquer and lavishly painted. Much of this went for export,

boosting both the town's prosperity and population throughout the 19th century, as the following table shows:

1801	12,566	1861	60,858
1811	14,836	1871	68,279
1821	18,386	1881	75,738
1831	24,732	1891	82,622
1841	36,382	1901	94,187
1851	49,989		

By 1850, Wolverhampton had become a specialist manufacturing centre for most items of ironmongery and almost all other goods made of iron, steel, brass

Below:
Wolverhampton viewed from the Penn Road about 1750. The Collegiate Church of St Peter dominates the skyline, centre left; and a number of chimneys foretell the town's illustrious industrial future, whilst the grazing sheep in the foreground are a reminder of its former importance as a wool market.
Author's Collection

or tin. In addition there were several large iron foundries, corn mills, about 20 malt kilns, two tanneries, and two extensive chemical works: William Bailey's, which made acids, and Mander, Weaver & Co, which produced paint, varnishes and medicines. There was also the largest artificial manure works in the country!

Industrial development on this scale brought many problems in its wake. The livelihood of so many was put at the mercy of the vicissitudes of trade such that when demand for iron fell following the Napoleonic Wars, by 1817 nearly half of Wolverhampton's iron smelting furnaces were blown out. Many faced near starvation, and hard times endured until demand for iron was rekindled by railway construction in the 1833-1846 period.

Overcrowding fostered unsanitary conditions, and many became dissatisfied with the Town Commissioners' abilty to deal with these, despite the provision of improvements such as gas lighting (1821), and a waterworks (1844). Accordingly, some of the town's leading ratepayers petitioned Queen Victoria to grant it a Charter of Incorporation as a Borough, which she did on 15 March 1848. A year later, 193 died of cholera. The new Town Council commissioned reports and embodied its plans in an Improvement Act which was passed in 1853. Much was remedied, but as a reporter from *The Builder* noted on a visit to Wolverhampton in 1860: 'In 10 years, with a rapidly increasing population, overlooked trifles grow into monster evils.'

A deep drainage and sewage scheme was implemented from 1861, and a plan was conceived to drive broad new streets through the worst areas to eradicate them and to replace the slum housing with new ones built elsewhere. Powers were obtained under an Artisans Dwellings and Street Improvements Act (1876); the new streets adding to Wolverhampton's already impressive building stock, the work of its leading architects who included Edward Banks, George Bidlake and George T. Robinson.

By 1900, the town's face had changed, as had its industry. Engineering firms had proliferated, and some of these had embraced motor cycle and car manufacture. Up to 1930, Wolverhampton rivalled Coventry and Birmingham as a centre for these trades; its famous makes including AJS motorcycles, Briton, Clyno, Guy, Star, Sunbeam and Turner cars; and Villiers motorcycle engines. The 1920s saw the biggest growth in their production, when nearly 31,000 was added to the population; and 1927 was the greatest year, when the Clyno was the third best selling car in Britain and Henry Seagrave became the first man to drive at over 200mph, in a Sunbeam. Despite this, within 5 years most of the town's car production had ceased, victim of the massive investment in plant made by Austin, Morris and by Fords.

Car production gave way to heavy industry in the 1930s, which saw the establishment of major companies in Wolverhampton, including Courtaulds, The Boulton Paul Aircraft Co, Goodyear Tyre & Rubber Co, Electric Construction Co and Star Aluminium to augment more established concerns like Chubb & Sons Lock & Safe Co and Mander Brothers. These firms' continued success ensured a steady surplus of employment in the town; which fared better than most until the economic recession hit the West Midlands hard in the late 1970s.

Transport in Wolverhampton before the Railway Age

1 — Roads

The Romans had driven their great highway — Watling Street — a few miles to the north of Wolverhampton, so it was not until the town developed as a major centre of the wool trade that its road system began to evolve. Then, a series of pack horse and cart tracks were driven by transporting wool from Shropshire, and the town's surrounding areas, for sale and transport on to the then important river port of Nottingham, en route to the Humber and the sea. As the wool trade declined, these same tracks served Wolverhampton's markets, and by the early 18th century a series of 10 roads radiated from the town centre, leading to Stafford, Cannock, Wednesfield, Willenhall, Bilston, Birmingham, Dudley, Penn, Compton and Tettenhall; names which they carry to this day.

During the last quarter of the 18th century, a number of turnpike trusts were set up to gate and levy tolls upon these roads to pay for their upkeep. A Wolverhampton Turnpike Trust was established to develop the road out through Tettenhall along the 26 miles to 'Shiffnal' in Shropshire. Tettenhall was also affected by the construction of the Wolverhampton section of the Holyhead Road. A rock cutting, completed in 1824, was required there; the whole road opening in 1828.

In the town itself, the first road improvements began in 1750 with the setting out of St James Square, a fashionable residential development, followed in 1755 by St John's Church and Square, which was laid out by the architect William Baker from designs for St Martin-in-the-Fields in London, on which he had worked as an assistant. In the same year, relocation of the Pig Market necessitated the driving of a connecting Market Street. Wolverhampton's first main thoroughfare, Queen Street, was laid out in 1788 and developed over the next 30 years; when, in 1820, it was joined by a road driven to link the town centre with the Tettenhall and Holyhead roads. Built on land purchased from Lord Darlington, this was called Darlington Street. Ten years later, a bypass, to keep Holyhead Road traffic from Bilston out of the town, was built on land bought from the Duke of Cleveland being called Cleveland Road and Cleveland Street. The 33 miles of roads in Wolverhampton was to grow to 166 miles within a century.

Most of the roads constructed then were surfaced with water-bonded macadam, which was looser than today's road surfaces and unsuited to either heavy loads or powered vehicles. Replacing this, laying down 22 miles of tramways, and building new roads to serve housing developments, kept the Town Council busy. A new main road to Birmingham was proposed in 1908, but was not fully surveyed until 1922. Construction began in 1924, and the 9¾-mile Birmingham New Road was opened by The Prince of Wales on 2 November 1927. Until the recent completion of the M54 to Telford, motorways missed Wolverhampton, unlike its Ring Road, which was first planned in 1951, but only finished in 1986.

2 — Canals

In 1717, Thomas Congreve proposed an 8-mile canal to link improved stretches of the rivers Stour and Penk, one of the country's first canal schemes, which would have involved extensive workings at Tettenhall; all part of an ambitious 70-mile scheme which was not built. The Staffordshire & Worcestershire Canal was the first to serve the town, passing within a mile of it to the west. This was sanctioned by an Act dated 14 May 1766, and opened south, to the River Severn, in 1770; and north in 1772. James Brindley was the engineer, and he built his first canal lock on this contract, at Compton, near Wolverhampton; the canal's summit also lying 1½ miles northwest of the town, at Autherley. Here there was to be a junction with a second Brindley-engineered canal, planned to link the Staffordshire & Worcestershire with Birmingham, which he had surveyed by June 1767. Brindley moved this junction slightly nearer to Wolverhampton at the confusingly-named Aldersley, near Bushbury; authority to build this, the Birmingham Canal being granted on 24 February 1768. It opened in stages from its Birmingham end from November 1769, skirting the eastern and northern sides of Wolverhampton and finally opening to Aldersley on 4 September 1772. Engineered to cut through as many coalfields as possible en route, coal was the principal traffic, but it also carried Smethwick sand and Rowley ragstone, all at a flat toll of 1½d per ton per mile. The canal proved a great stimulus to the area's mining and industry, many local firms can date their prosperity from its opening.

The movement of coal was also the reason for a third canal, the Wyrley & Essington, which was authorised on 30 April 1792, and engineered by W. Pitt. This opened in 1797, passing through the mining areas of Essington Wood, Great Wyrley, Bloxwich and Willenhall, before terminating in the Birmingham Canal at extensive wharfs built on the eastern side of Wolverhampton in Horseley Fields.

For the next 30 years these three canals, with extensions and improvements, formed the basic pattern of waterways serving Wolverhampton. In 1824, Thomas Telford began work to straighten the Birmingham Canal, and in 1825 he became engineer to a new line: The Birmingham & Liverpool Junction (later the Shropshire Union) Canal. By an Act of 26 May 1826, this commenced at the summit of the Staffordshire & Worcestershire near Tettenhall and proceeded to a junction with the Ellesmere & Chester Canals near Nantwich in Cheshire; providing an important link between the industries of south Staffordshire and Chester, Liverpool and north Wales.

Passenger boats also plied their way along Wolverhampton's canals; the most celebrated of these 'swift packets' being the *Euphrates*, operated by Thomas Monk between the town and nearby Tipton from July 1830 onwards. Drawn by two trotting horses, one mounted, these vessels proved more popular with their passengers than with the canal companies due to the damage their considerable wake did to the canal bank. Despite such opposition, swift packets continued, being extended to Dudley and Birmingham. The full journey took 2hr 10min, a seat in the second class cabin costing 1s, one in the best cabin 1s 4d; but within two years these boats had ceased to work, victims of the opening of a more direct railway link between Wolverhampton and Birmingham.

Railways were to hit the bulk of Wolverhampton's other canal traffic. By 1860, the greater proportion of this went by rail, and some canal branches and wharfs were closed. A decline to extinction seemed inevitable, aided by the Birmingham Canal leaking badly where it crossed former mineworkings, and portions of the South Staffordshire coalfield becoming exhausted. Ironically, the canals were saved by the railway companies, which used them as collecting agencies. Some coal traffic returned during World War 1, but by the 1920s further collieries were exhausted, and some ironworks closed, leaving the canals unfit to fend off competition from road transport. But for remaining short-haul workings to serve local power stations, none of Wolverhampton's canals would have survived to enjoy control under the British Waterways Board, and welcome attention from canal trusts.

3 — Public transport

Wolverhampton's first regular daily coach service was to neighbouring Walsall. This began in July 1783, and was joined in 1787 by a thrice-weekly

service to London via Birmingham. By 1808, the town was on the route of the London to Holyhead 'Irish Mail' coaches and 10 years later it boasted services to Bristol, Liverpool, Chester and Manchester. Over the next 20 years, the number of coach services proliferated. A Wolverhampton directory of 1834 lists no fewer than 31. The choice was bewildering. To London, one could take the *Triumph*, *Rocket*, *Wonder*, *Nimrod* or *RobRoy*; to Birmingham there was the *Phoenix*, *Erin-go-Brough*, *Eclipse*, *Hero* or *Harkforward*, or to Bridgnorth *The Shropshire Hero*. Most of these names were chosen to suggest speed, which could hardly be said of *The Everlasting* to Bristol. But who could resist riding *The Bang-up* all the way to Liverpool?

Coach services declined in the face of railway competition from 1837 onwards, thereafter concentrating on local trips until these too were overtaken by an expansion in local rail services in the 1852-54 period. The end was sudden. An 1855 directory lists only the service to Bridgnorth, which was not to see any railway competition for almost half a century. On shorter journeys, Wolverhampton's coaches also faced competition from private horsebuses, the first

of which began operating to Darlaston in 1833, with a Birmingham via Dudley service commencing in 1835. These, and other operators, actually benefited from the opening of the Grand Junction Railway's Wolverhampton station in July 1837, as this lay 1½ miles distant from the town centre, at Wednesfield Heath; a trend reversed when the more centrally-located General and Joint stations opened in 1852 and 1854 respectively.

A few of Wolverhampton's horse omnibus services survived beyond the introduction of horse trams in May 1878, but could not match the latter in frequency and low fares. Three basic tram routes were constructed, to Tettenhall, Willenhall and Bilston; but this system was expanded when the tramways were electrified from February 1902. A disdain for overhead wires led to the adoption of the Lorain surface contact system of current collection which, inside 20 years, proved unreliable and costly to maintain. It was therefore replaced by the more conventional overhead wires by October 1921. Eager to replace its ageing tramcar fleet, the town's Transport Department experimented with trolleybus operation in March 1923. This proved so successful that the Wednesfield tram route was converted to trolleybus operation that July. Other routes followed until the last, that to Bilston, saw its last tram on 30 November 1928.

Wolverhampton so took to trolleybuses that by 1929 it had the largest system in the world, which brought many visits to the town from other public transport operators at home and abroad. These familiar apple green and primrose vehicles served the town well, until they too were replaced by motor buses in a conversion programme that began on 9 June 1963, and ended with the closure of the Dudley route on 5 March 1967. Then, on 1 October 1969, Wolverhampton's buses came under the control of the West Midlands Passenger Transport Authority, ending 70 years of municipal transport operation in the town.

2: The 'North Western' Lines to 1962

The first railway to serve Wolverhampton was owned and operated for the longest period by the London & North Western Railway (LNWR). This chapter considers that line, and the others serving the town that were associated with that company.

Early Proposals 1806-1831

If one draws a straight line between Birmingham and Liverpool or Chester it passes very close to Wolverhampton. In essence, this is how a railway first came to serve the town. As we have seen, by 1800 the Wolverhampton area was well served by roads and canals which facilitated local transport; yet links to more distant regions, notably the industry and ports of the Northwest, were poor. The Wyrley & Essington Canal was still 25 years away, and whilst railways were only in their infancy, they had their advocates, like William James, who in 1806 proposed a line of 'engine railroad' extending northwest from Birmingham, passing through Wednesbury en route to the Staffordshire coalfields.

Railways also had their detractors, who saw the technology involved as unproven, and James' scheme was not implemented, but others followed; underlining a growing dissatisfaction with the capacity of the roads and canals in the Wolverhampton area. Elsewhere in the country, notably in the Northeast, a succession of colliery railways had opened from 1812 onwards, demonstrating the potential of both railways and the steam locomotives that worked them. By 1822 interest had been rekindled in a West Midlands-Northwest rail link. Independently, groups of businessmen in Birmingham and Liverpool began to plan the construction of a railway to link the two places; and, hearing of each other sometime in 1823, formed a joint committee for 'making a railroad from the town of Birmingham, through the Staffordshire collieries and ironworks, by Wolverhampton, Nantwich and Chester to the River Mersey at Birkenhead, opposite Liverpool — the line to be known as the Birmingham & Liverpool Railroad Co' (B&L).

A Bill to sanction the construction of the line was heard in the 1824 Parliamentary session, but was heavily defeated by the combined opposition of canal proprietors and landowners, who had also woken up to railways' potential. Given new heart by the opening of the Stockton & Darlington Railway in September 1825, the B&L group tried again in 1826,

but was even more heavily defeated. Four years elapsed before the success of the Liverpool & Manchester Railway gave the public perception of railways a great fillip.

Both the Birmingham and Liverpool committees were revived, each working on half the line, which was resurveyed. Three engineers were appointed, with George Stephenson, star of the Liverpool & Manchester line, in overall charge; Joseph Locke, a Stephenson protégé, tackling the northern section, and John Urpeth Rastrick, designer of the Chillington ironworks at Wolverhampton, responsible for the southern section. Two bills, one for each section, were presented to the 1830 Parliamentary session; the southern one being rejected out of hand and the northern one being lost through the dissolution of Parliament following the rejection of the Reform Bill.

The Grand Junction Railway

By 1831 the B&L scheme must have seemed ill-starred, but circumstances had changed. That year saw the Warrington & Newton Railway open; a southward spur off the Liverpool & Manchester line, and the revival of a scheme for another long line to link London and Birmingham, later to be the London & Birmingham Railway (L&B). And so, someone thought, if the Warrington & Newton line was extended a little further south it could join the proposed B&L line, thus linking all three regions. Then, if the London to Birmingham line was built, the B&L line would serve to unite the nation's capital with its most important industrial areas and port. New plans were prepared incorporating these ideas, which were also reflected in the adoption of a new name for the line: The Grand Junction Railway (GJR).

Planning and construction

Engineering duties for the newly-styled line remained in the hands of Stephenson, Locke and Rastrick; the latter completing his survey and estimate for the southern portion of the line on 9 February 1831. It was to cost £1 million, or £20,000

Right:
How the LNWR saw Wolverhampton . . . as part of Birmingham apparently! This 1915 map shows Wolverhampton's 'North Western' lines and stations prior to any major closures. *Railway Magazine*

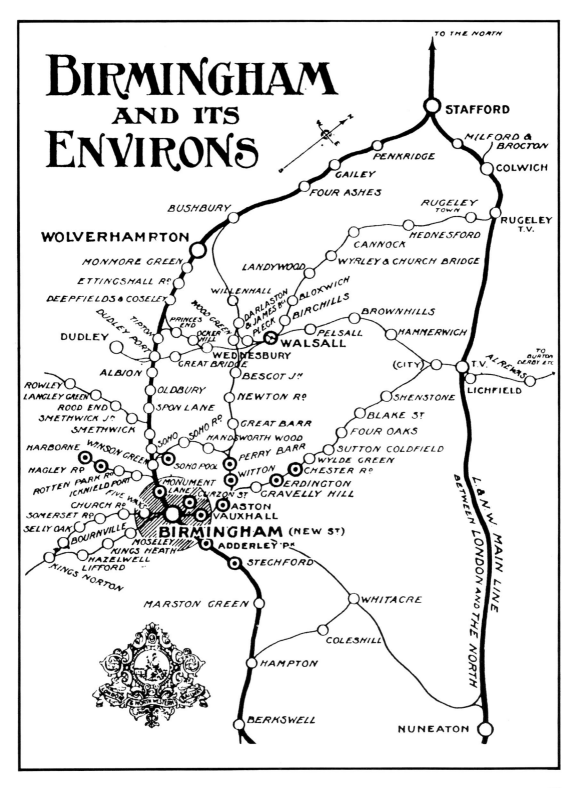

BIRMINGHAM
AND ITS
ENVIRONS

TO THE NORTH

STAFFORD

MILFORD & BROCTON

COLWICH

PENKRIDGE

GAILEY

FOUR ASHES

RUGELEY
TOWN

RUGELEY
T.V.

BUSHBURY

HEDNESFORD

WOLVERHAMPTON

CANNOCK

MONMORE GREEN

LANDYWOOD

WYRLEY & CHURCH BRIDGE

ETTINGSHALL RD.

WILLENHALL

DEEPFIELDS & COSELEY

BLOXWICH

WOOD GREEN

BROWNHILLS

DARLASTON
& JAMES BR.

BIRCHILLS

HAMMERWICH

PLECK

DUDLEY PORT

PRINCES
END

TIPTON

OCKER
HILL

PELSALL

DUDLEY

WALSALL

(CITY)

TO
BURTON
DERBY ETC.

WEDNESBURY

T.V.

ALREWAS

GREAT BRIDGE

ALBION

BESCOT JN.

LICHFIELD

OLDBURY

NEWTON RD.

SHENSTONE

ROWLEY
LANGLEY GREEN

SPON LANE

ROOD END

GREAT BARR

BLAKE ST.

SMETHWICK JN.

SOHO

SOHO RD.

FOUR OAKS

SMETHWICK

HANDSWORTH WOOD

HARBORNE

WINSON GREEN

PERRY BARR

SUTTON COLDFIELD

HAGLEY RD.

SOHO POOL

WYLDE GREEN

ROTTEN PARK RD.

WITTON

CHESTER RD.

ICKNIELD PORT

MONUMENT
LANE

ERDINGTON

FIVE WAYS

CURZON ST.

GRAVELLY HILL

CHURCH RD.

ASTON

SOMERSET RD.

VAUXHALL

SELLY OAK

BIRMINGHAM (NEW ST.)

BOURNVILLE

MOSELEY

ADDERLEY PK.

KINGS HEATH

HAZELWELL

STECHFORD

LIFFORD

KINGS NORTON

MARSTON GREEN

WHITACRE

COLESHILL

HAMPTON

L. & N.W. MAIN LINE
BETWEEN LONDON AND THE NORTH

BERKSWELL

NUNEATON

13

per mile, and included a 2-mile branch to Wolverhampton at a cost of £43,507 4s. The 219-clause Grand Junction Act received the Royal Assent on 6 May 1833, the same day as the L&B Act, work beginning on the line's construction immediately.

A series of disagreements ensued, seeing first Rastrick resign in September 1833, followed exactly two years later by Stephenson, leaving Locke in overall charge. The southern end of the line presented the most engineering difficulties which were not aided by a number of changes to the route. One involved Rastrick's proposed branch to serve Wolverhampton town centre, sanctioned by an Act of 16 June 1834 but not built; another, the approach to Birmingham, which had to be altered by an Act of 12 June 1835 following objections from James Watt's son, the resident of Aston Hall.

More engineering difficulties were encountered near the site of the Wolverhampton station at Wednesfield Heath. Here a deep cutting and short 186yd tunnel were required, and north of this a series of shallow cuttings and embankments were needed. Progress on the whole line was very patchy and reflected these difficulties. By November 1834, all of the northern section contracts had been let, but none of the southern ones. Work proceeded throughout 1835. On 9 March 1836 a contract to supply the railway with 500 tons of rails and chairs was awarded to Wolverhampton's Chillington ironworks, and on 31 August 1836 the first locomotives were ordered.

Opening

The GJR was completed between Liverpool and Wolverhampton by the end of May 1837, and on 1 June a Director's train covered the 83 miles in 3½hr. A second run, this time to the temporary Birmingham terminus at Vauxhall, was made on 24 June, with a further Director's train running on 1 July, just prior to the public opening on 4 July.

Official ceremony was subdued. King George IV had died on 20 June and was not to be buried until 8 July. Some of the Directors had also been present at the opening of the Liverpool & Manchester Railway and had witnessed the fatal accident to William Huskisson, an advocate of the line, and past whose birthplace the line travelled. Not wishing to see such scenes repeated they simply opened the doors for business. The public were a little more appreciative of the occasion's significance. At Birmingham the 7.00am departure of the first train deterred few and by 6.00am the station approach was choked with people. Crowds lined the route between Birmingham and Wolverhampton, and whilst the first train attained speeds of up to 40mph between these towns, subsequent trains were delayed by hordes of people on the line, the driver of the second train forgetting to stop at Wolverhampton (a precedent indeed).

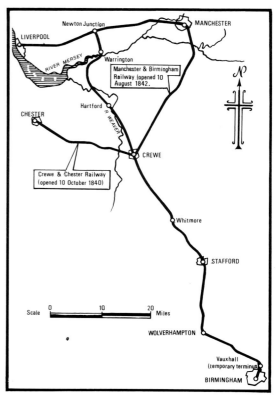

Above:
The Grand Junction Railway, as opened on 4 July 1837, showing the additional lines built prior to the formation of the LNWR.

The Wolverhampton station

The Wolverhampton Grand Junction station stood about a mile northeast of the town centre at Wednesfield Heath; being situated at the end of a 300yd long deep cutting that commences at the northern portal of the 186yd Summit Tunnel, the highest point on the line. It did not open with the rest of the line as its platforms were not completed in time, possibly, as a later plan reveals, because here, as elsewhere along the GJR line, the company did not acquire title to the land it occupied until after it had opened.

Wolverhampton was designated as a principal or 'First Class' station by the GJR, although, at least initially, its facilities were modest by present-day standards. The station building was undistinguished, a small rectangular structure with more than a hint of canal architecture about it, to which facilities were gradually added, as chronicled in a series of guides to the line published between 1837 and 1842. To begin with, Osborne noted: 'a neat and commodious office for the reception of passengers and the transaction of business, and a private room for females'; all of the engines being 'supplied with water and coke', examined and their wheels greased. Yet by 1839, Roscoe found that:

'This station forms a very extensive and important commercial depot . . . . This is plainly discovered by the capacious warehouses which have been formed for the transaction of business — its ample engine house, and the substantial and convenient buildings which have been erected for the residence of the agent and the policeman attached to this part of the line. Here . . . is an excellent booking office, and private waiting rooms appropriated to both the sexes. The first-class train remains at this station for nearly ten minutes, during which time it takes breath, and draws in a supply of water, through a series of leathern tubes connected with a reservoir supplied from the Wyrley & Essington canal.'

One year later, Mogg observed that: 'the Wolverhampton station is a large establishment . . . here warehouses for goods, workshops, smithies and sheds, the latter for the reception and reparation of engines have been erected, and refreshment and retiring rooms, with every requisite, have been provided . . . . Here the carriages undergo an inspection and the engines are invigorated'. An 1842 guide further informs us that the engine house

'holds two or three engines'. In addition there was the stationmaster's house, which may have been the 'agent's house' noted by Roscoe; plus a row of cottages, originally erected to house the navvies building Summit Tunnel, which may have been the policeman's residence Roscoe mentions.

Following the opening of the Wolverhampton General (High Level) station on 24 June 1852, trains continued to call at the GJR station. It was renamed Wednesfield Heath in November 1852, and closed completely on 1 September 1853; reopening to serve local trains only between 1 August 1855 and 1 January 1873, but remaining open for goods and parcels until 4 October 1965.

Early train services

The 14½ miles of the GJR between Birmingham and Wolverhampton had no fewer than five intermediate stations: at Perry Barr, Newton Road, Bescot Bridge, James Bridge and Willenhall; more than on any other stretch of the line between two first-class stations. Upon opening there were six trains per day in each direction; the Birmingham departures being at 7.00am, 8.30am, 11.30am, 2.30pm, 4.30pm and 7.00pm. All were of first-class coaches, with only the second and fifth of these including second-class accommodation. First-class trains only stopped at first-class stations; mixed trains stopped at every station. There was also a Wolverhampton train which left there at 8.00am, returning from Birmingham at 7.00pm. On Sundays, only first-class trains ran, carrying second-class accommodation but only stopping at first-class stations. The fares were: Wolverhampton to Birmingham, first-class 2/6, second-class 1/6 (taking 40min and 56min respectively); Birmingham to Liverpool or Manchester, first-class £1 1s 0d, second-class 14/- (taking 4½hr and 5hr 24min respectively).

Below:
The first Wolverhampton station, on the Grand Junction Railway. This undistinguished single-storey building was one of the GJR's first-class stations and is seen here in 1967 after closure as a goods station. The house on the right once belonged to the stationmaster.
Wolverhampton Library

An intensive coach and omnibus service developed to take passengers alighting at Wolverhampton to the town, two coaches also acting as shuttles to ferry people to the coaching inns for coaches to Worcester, Shrewsbury, Bridgnorth and Stourbridge. With the opening of the London & Birmingham Railway on 17 September 1838, the GJR timetable was recast to provide some connecting services, but with minor alterations, such as extending the Wolverhampton local train to run to and from Stafford, the service on the line remained much as described; unlike the fares. The GJR pioneered the use of low fares to attract passengers, introducing these on Wolverhampton Races trains from 3 August 1841; Wolverhampton station becoming a special low fare station in 1842, first-class travel then costing only 2d per mile.

The Shrewsbury & Birmingham Railway

The opening of the L&B also began a curious relationship between that company and the GJR. A measure of co-operation was required to satisfy passenger demand for through travel from London and the Northwest; but this was difficult to achieve, and so both parties were always on the lookout for newly promoted lines running north or south in which they could invest with an eye to future use. One such line was the Shrewsbury & Birmingham Railway (S&B), which, although eventually to be absorbed by the Great Western Railway (GWR), was to have a considerable impact upon the activities of the LNWR both in Wolverhampton and nationally.

Early schemes 1830-1844

Proposals to link Shrewsbury with Birmingham by rail were first put forward in 1830, and repeated more or less biannually thereafter. An 1836 attempt was the first to prepare an engineer's report, one in 1839 the first to present a bill before Parliament; neither succeeded. Another attempt was made in 1842, when a scheme to connect Shrewsbury with the GJR line at Wolverhampton was proposed. In 1843, having failed to secure the GJR's interest in this, the scheme was altered to include construction of a separate line between Wolverhampton and Birmingham, which greatly interested the L&B, which offered to lease it upon completion.

A provisional committee of the 'Shrewsbury & Wolverhampton Dudley & Birmingham Railway Co' was formed in February 1844, resulting in the submission to Parliament of a Bill to construct the line that November. This received its first reading on 16 February 1845, and was opposed by the GJR. On 18 February a pro-Grand Junction MP, suitably primed, pointed out that the Bill was in breach of the rules on standing orders governing the submission of railway bills to the House. A list of buildings situated between Birmingham and Wolverhampton

was missing from the plans. This should have shown the names of the landowners affected by the proposed line and whether they assented, dissented or were neutral in respect of the compulsory purchase of their land. In fact such breaches of procedure were common, but once pointed out they could not be ignored. The whole matter was referred to the Commons Select Committee on Standing Orders. Before this met on 3 March, the Shrewsbury line's proposers began to panic. A delegation went cap in hand to the Grand Junction Railway to try and revitalise the link with its line, this time at Willenhall; talks ensued. By 7 March the Standing Orders Select Committee recommended that the Bill be withdrawn as 'inadmissible'; and by 18 March negotiations with the GJR company were written off as 'useless'. Legal counsel continued to act for the Shrewsbury line, but on 30 May the proposers gave up and applied to get the deposit on their Bill repaid.

The formation of the London & North Western Railway

Bloodied but unbowed, the promoters of the Shrewsbury to Birmingham line had at least begun to learn the rules of the railway promotion game.

The spate of railway promotion in 1844 that marked the beginning of the period known as the Railway Mania, forced both the GJR and L&B companies to accept that they could not reasonably expect to retain their monopolies of lines serving London, Birmingham and the Northwest for much longer. Accordingly, early in that year they concluded an agreement which stated that they would 'remain separate and distinct as at present, but shall unite for mutual protection'; followed by a number of clearly worded examples stating instances of conflicting interest and what each company would do or not do in return for corresponding action from the other. One such example concerned the Shrewsbury line, stating that if the L&B withdrew its offer to lease this upon completion, the GJR would build its own line to Wolverhampton, guaranteeing the promoters a dividend upon their original investment in return for a perpetual lease of the line. Unfortunately, in a matter of weeks both parties were accusing the other of breaching this agreement.

Many involved in these disputes grew weary of them. Matters came to a head at the summer half-yearly meetings of both companies, held in early August 1845, at which the shareholders, many of whom held shares in each company, pressed for the disputes between the two to cease. Talks began, and by the end of October an agreement to amalgamate had been finalised. Pending the passing of an Act of Parliament to formally sanction their amalgamation, the two companies began to function as one from 1 January 1846. All previous agreements made by one or the other with regard to supporting new lines were cancelled. On 16 July 1846, the Royal

Assent was given to the Act of amalgamation, formally constituting the two companies as one: the LNWR.

The inception of the Shrewsbury & Birmingham Railway

Within five weeks of the abandonment of the previous Bill, a new provisional committee of the Shrewsbury and Wolverhampton, Dudley & Birmingham Railway was formed on 2 July 1845. Meeting that day, certain changes were planned. The recently-failed Bill had been based upon the 1839 plans, themselves based upon the 1836 engineer's report. In view of the close scrutiny they now knew railway plans to receive, a new survey and set of plans was ordered. Robert Stephenson was approached to survey the line and superintend its construction, and, at his behest, William Baker, a Stephenson disciple, was appointed company engineer. Stephenson began work almost immediately, surveying the railway's course on horseback from the Shrewsbury end. On 16 August several of the company's Directors attended him at Oakengates to hear his progress, and he completed the survey in late September.

Money was short. The cost of the abortive Bill and new survey reduced already depleted reserves, forcing the company to seek ways of further reducing its committed expenditure. With a new Bill to be deposited at the House of Commons by 30 November, drastic measures were needed, and it was decided to split the cost of constructing the line. From 1 October, the section of the line between Shrewsbury and Wolverhampton was referred to as 'the new line', and that between Wolverhampton and Birmingham as the Stour Valley Railway. This was to be a new company to be funded equally by public subscriptions, the Shrewsbury line, the L&B, and the Birmingham Canal Co; taking its now familiar title from a planned branch along the valley of the River Stour, from Smethwick to Stourbridge and Stourport.

On 1 January 1846, the Shrewsbury & Wolverhampton Dudley & Birmingham Railway Company changed its title to the simpler Shrewsbury & Birmingham Railway Company (S&B), already inaccurate; and the Stour Valley line became known as the Birmingham Wolverhampton & Stour Valley Railway Co (Stour Valley). The same day, the L&B company withdrew its support for the Stour Valley line, in accordance with the terms of its amalgamation with the GJR. The L&B likewise withdrew its support from the company it had set up under the terms of the 1844 agreement to build its own line to Wolverhampton: the Shrewsbury Wolverhampton & South Staffordshire Junction Railway.

The year 1846 had not begun well. The new S&B company had lost a quarter of the capital it needed to build its line into Birmingham (£190,087 in 1846 alone), and faced a similarly under-funded competitor seeking Parliamentary approval to build a line along the same route as its own. Agreement was found in a Committee Room of the House of Commons, where arbitration determined that the S&B should build its line by virtue of having applied to do so before, and that its Bill should be amended to include an amalgamation with the Shrewsbury Wolverhampton & South Staffordshire Junction Co, which would lose its power to raise capital. At the 11th hour, this Bill was further amended to make construction of the section of the line between Shrewsbury and Wellington the joint responsibility of the company and the newly formed 'Shrewsbury & Birmingham & Shropshire Union Railways & Canal Co' (Shropshire Union). This was a joint speculative venture of the United Ellesmere & Chester, Shrewsbury, and Montgomery Canal companies, which planned to convert 155 miles of their canals into railways.

Thus heavily amended, but unopposed, the S&B Act received the Royal Assent on 3 August 1846, along with Acts authorising the Stour Valley and Shropshire Union lines. Of the 42¾ miles originally proposed, 10½ miles were to be built jointly with the Shropshire Union company, and 12¾ by the Stour Valley company, leaving just 19½ miles. The S&B had become the 'Wellington & Wolverhampton' railway, with only an additonal 4-mile branch from Wellington to the Dawley ironworks at Lightmoor; and a short spur to Victoria Basin in Wolverhampton to its name. Yet, however emasculated it had become, the S&B was, in its brief period of independence, to set the pattern of Wolverhampton's railways for the next century or so.

The construction of the Shrewsbury & Birmingham Railway

At a meeting held on 19 September 1846 the Directors of the S&B announced that they had possession of all the land they required between Wellington and Oakengates, and that work on constructing the line was to start there first as it was, with a tunnel at Oakengates, the heaviest on the line. However, by 27 March 1847 only the contract for the joint Shrewsbury to Wellington section had been let; and it was not until early May that year that the contract for the Wellington to Wolverhampton section was taken. Even then, progress was slow. On 4 September 1847 the *Railway Times* noted that 'most of the heavy works on the line have been commenced and are in a rapid course of execution, except those at Oxley', but on 11 September corrected this to 'only the works at Oxley have been commenced'.

The year 1848 saw steady progress. On 26 May Edward Banks, Wolverhampton's leading architect, was appointed architect and surveyor to the company, and instructed to superintend the erection

Above:
Sprinter set No 150103 draws into Oakengates station on the S&B line on 22 August 1988. Oakengates was one of the original S&B stations. Designed by the company's Architect, Edward Banks, it is the only one surviving built in the white brick used for the original High Level station and the company offices. *Author*

of all the company's buildings; and on 29 November the first two S&B railway carriages were displayed at the LNWR Wolverhampton station at Wednesfield Heath. These had been made by the Bromsgrove Railway & Carriage Co and bore a livery of lake lined out with a rich dark blue. The company also announced that further carriages, then being manufactured in Wolverhampton by William Tudor at his Cleveland Road premises, were almost ready for use; and that when completed all of the carriages were to be used on the Shrewsbury & Chester line until the S&B opened. By 9 February 1849, William Baker reported that the works from Shrewsbury to Oakengates were 'rapidly drawing to a close', and tenders for building the stations, sheds and goods warehouses at Oakengates, Shifnal, Albrighton and Codsall were first advertised on 9 March 1849, the contracts being let by the beginning of April.

The opening of the Shrewsbury & Birmingham Railway and the temporary Wolverhampton station

The Shrewsbury to Wellington section of the S&B opened on 1 June 1849; the opening of the rest of the line being delayed by construction work on the 471yd tunnel at Oakengates. This remaining section opened on 12 November 1849 to a temporary station at Wolverhampton, the contract for the main station there not having been let until May that year.

Much mystery has surrounded this temporary station over the ensuing years. Contrary to popular belief, it was situated on the Wednesfield Road, and was built at a cost of £380, consisting of a main building and a single platform at a higher level on the embankment carrying the main S&B running lines towards the Wolverhampton General station. A separate loading area, served by double tracks, was also provided; possibly for the loading and unloading of carriages. The temporary station was used until the opening of the General station on 24 June 1852, after which it was sold to the Shropshire Union Canal company, serving as a stable block and general storehouse until it was demolished in the late 1970s as part of Wolverhampton's ring road development.

The Birmingham Wolverhampton & Stour Valley Railway

Although the S&B had originally agreed to the idea of building the Wolverhampton to Birmingham section of its line jointly with another railway company to save money, this move well suited the motives of the LNWR. As the formation of the latter approached, the Birmingham termini of the GJR and L&B were situated side by side at Curzon Street, over half a mile from the town centre. With news that the GWR's Birmingham station was to be built on Snow Hill, in the heart of the town's commercial district, the two companies planned their own station on a vast site of derelict housing adjoining Navigation Street, requiring a ¾ mile extension of the line. Whilst this new station's position would be more advantageous, it would also lengthen the existing journey to Wolverhampton, itself to have a more centrally located station built by the S&B company, which also planned to build a direct line from there to Birmingham. By assisting the S&B company with this line, the LNWR could both split the cost of building a line it needed to build in any case and control who had use of this and who gained access to

In later years Deepfields station was renamed Coseley & Deepfields and as such is seen here on Sunday 5 June 1965 as a double-headed Birmingham-bound Glasgow-Edinburgh train, hauled by sister locomotives D375 (40175) and D332 (40132), passes the now demolished down platform buildings. *Michael Mensing*

its new Navigation Street station. But the greatest fears of the LNWR concerned the spread of the GWR, which was, via interests in a number of lines, then converging upon Wolverhampton.

The Stour Valley Railway was sanctioned on 3 August 1846 and construction began immediately from the Birmingham end, being divided into three sections: Birmingham to Winson Green, which included an 845yd tunnel approach to Navigation Street; Winson Green to Oldbury and from there to Bushbury. In 1847 the LNWR strengthened its control of the line. Firstly, it took over the Birmingham Canal, adding its quarter share to the LNWR's own moribund investment. Secondly, it leased the line under the terms of an Act passed on 1 July that also formally gave the S&B use of it unless it became 'leased to, or purchased by, or amalgamated with, the Great Western' or any of its associated companies. Thirdly, a further Act of 9 July made the Wolverhampton General station, and the line from there to Bushbury, joint property with the S&B company.

Control of the Stour Valley line thus secured, its construction proceeded at a more leisurely pace; the years 1848, 1849 and 1850 passing without it opening. One cause of delay was work on the Birmingham approach tunnel, and when the line was eventually inspected and declared ready to open, on 21 November 1851, it was only to be worked between Wolverhampton and the station at Monument Lane, just beyond this tunnel's mouth. The opening was

announced for 1 December, the S&B company expecting finally to run its trains through to Birmingham from that date.

Unfortunately, as we shall see, in May 1851 the S&B had concluded an agreement to amalgamate with the GWR in the future, in 1856 or 1857. And so the LNWR invoked the terms of its 1847 agreement with the S&B company, stressing the words 'amalgamate with' and 'GWR'; the S&B countering by stressing the word 'future'. The scene was thus set for a protracted legal and physical battle.

The Stour Valley line eventually opened to goods traffic on 1 February 1852, and to passengers (to a temporary platform just inside the Navigation Street site) on 1 July 1852, with stations at Smethwick, Spon Lane, Oldbury & Bromford Lane, Dudley Port, Tipton, Deepfields and Ettingshall Road & Bilston. Additional stations were opened at Bushbury (2 August 1852), Albion (1 May 1853), Monument Lane (1 July 1854), and Monmore Green (1 December 1863). Birmingham New Street, so named from 1 November 1852, opened fully on 1 June 1854.

The legal, financial and other difficulties of the S&B

The S&B Act authorised the company to raise £1.3 million, giving powers to borrow a further £433,333. Yet, within a short period its activities had become so complicated that this sum was seen as being woefully inadequate. To start with it had become committed to contribute towards the building of three main line stations. In addition to the Wolverhampton General station (later the High Level) on 29 August 1846, the S&B took a quarter share in the cost of building the General station at Shrewsbury, which opened on 12 October 1848, and had, by 1852, cost the company £28,400. The cost of the Wolverhampton General station was shared with the LNWR from July 1847, but by the time it opened in 1852 this half share had cost £63,570. Then, on 14 August 1848, the company became a one-third partner with the Oxford Worcester & Wolverhampton and Birmingham Wolverhampton & Dudley companies in the building of the Wolverhampton Joint station (later the Low Level), at an estimated contribution of £167,000.

Not surprisingly, extra capital had to be raised, which was done by two further share issues in August 1847 and September 1848, each netting £155,000. One of the biggest drains upon resources were the legal fees incurred in obtaining the Parliamentary Act and in pursuing previously-agreed rights with the LNWR. By the end of 1848, £79,920 had been spent on this alone; and it was just the beginning. In December 1850 the S&B company began legal action to prevent the LNWR from poaching its local traffic, and in August 1851 it began its longest legal battle, to gain the right to use the Wolverhampton General station and Stour Valley line, which was not to be satisfactorily resolved until 29 May 1854.

If all of this was not bad enough, events could sometimes take a violent turn. Perhaps the most celebrated occasions were the so-called 'Battles of Wolverhampton'; the first of which took place on Saturday 13 July 1850, when the S&B was forcibly prevented from laying a siding to the Birmingham Canal, and the second of which took place on Monday 1 December 1851. Upon hearing that the opening of the Stour Valley line had been announced, an S&B official declared: 'We shall stand no humbug; we shall run to Birmingham', and although the opening was suddenly rescinded late on 30 November the S&B company was undaunted. At 9.05am the next day one of its trains set off for

Birmingham, only to be arrested a few yards on by signals and the explosion of a dozen detonators; coming to a halt buffer to buffer with an LNWR locomotive, one of which had been placed on each track at the limit of Stour Valley property, guarded by a hundred men. In addition, ¼-mile nearer Birmingham, another locomotive was derailed and lengths of rail were taken up to qualify the closure of the line as 'through an accident'. Witnessed by some 5,000 people, the S&B locomotive was coupled to one of the LNWR ones in an abortive attempt to drag it out of the way. A riot was only avoided by the personal intervention of the Mayor and police chief of Wolverhampton; all parties adjourning to the Town Hall where assurances were given that it would not happen again.

This dispute did not only involve railway officials. From the opening of the Wolverhampton General station the staff there were under orders not to assist passengers travelling on S&B tickets. Their antics are best described by the following letter to the *Birmingham Journal* from one Charles Sturge, relating events of 26 December 1853.

'I arrived at the Wolverhampton station about a quarter before ten on Monday night . . . and immediately inquired if the last Stour Valley train had left. The reply was that it had not yet

Below:
GWR No 40 was formerly S&B No 6, and carried the distinction of being the longest surviving of all the S&B locomotives, not being withdrawn until January 1904; by which time it had been rebuilt three times, and probably did not have any of the original engine left in it at all! *Bucknall Collection/Ian Allan Library*

arrived. I went at once to the Booking Office, but was refused tickets with a sneer. This occurred eleven minutes before the train started, and a number of passengers who applied afterwards were allowed to proceed by this train. I then entreated different parties wearing the LNWR badge to allow us to enter the train, as there was plenty of room . . . but was answered "I cannot. It is contrary to positive orders" . . . . I applied to the first official I could meet with for a special train . . . (but) he shortly returned to us in the second-class refreshment room, where the porters were enjoying a good supper (my wife had previously asked to be admitted to the ladies' waiting room to no purpose), with a person who said that it was by his orders that we were refused tickets, and that we should not have a special train, and persisted in his refusal, although I offered him £20 for it. I am sure there was nothing personal in all this. I am bound to add, that at half-past eleven o'clock the same individual came to us, and said they were about to send a train of empty carriages to Birmingham in which we proceeded at seventeen minutes before midnight.'

It is therefore little wonder that, in the face of such concerted opposition, the S&B listened with interest

Below:
The frontage of Wolverhampton High Level in 1907, showing its main architectural features. The three railway company nameboards indicate its dual usage by the LNWR and Midland companies, and directs GWR passengers to the subway leading to the Low Level station. *Wolverhampton Library*

to approaches from the GWR; an ally equal to the task of resisting the LNWR. The S&B had made an initial approach on 5 December 1847, when much of the above lay in the future, and had been politely declined. But the establishment of a joint committee, following the signing of a traffic agreement on 10 January 1851, led to an offer to amalgamate with the GWR in 1856 or 1857 which was agreed on 8 May that year. The S&B weakened by its fight with the LNWR, brought this forward and it became effective from 1 September 1854.

The Shrewsbury & Birmingham's golden summer, 1854

Amalgamation with the GWR agreed, problems with the LNWR resolved, the S&B enjoyed just over nine months of what might have been — running its trains over the Stour Valley line into Birmingham New Street, between 4 February and 13 November 1854. The latter date was via an extension of running powers granted by the LNWR following the collapse of a bridge on the GWR line at Handsworth on 23 August.

The High Level station

The first indication of the site of the Wolverhampton General station was given in *The Builder* on 13 September 1845, which announced: 'It is the determination of several railway companies whose lines pass through Wolverhampton to unite in the erection of one grand station as near the centre of that town as possible. The bottom of Queen Street is the spot named for the joint terminus.' On 3 June 1846, the *Wolverhampton Chronicle* carried a feature headed 'The Wolverhampton Railway Station', which provided clear evidence that this was

passenger footbridge, new platforms and buildings on the up side, separate goods lines, and improved refreshment room facilities; including the package in its New Lines &c Bill for 1876. Unfortunately,

asked the LMS to build a new High Level station to provide work for the unemployed, but it declined. Unaffected by wartime bombing, High Level passed into British Railways ownership in 1948, remaining unaltered until its rebuilding was announced in

Left:
From this 1908 view of the High Level station interior it is clear how it was possible for the first-ever platform ticket machine installed upon the LNWR to have taken over £43 in its first month. There is also a wealth of detail in this photograph, especially of the carriage roofs. *Bennett Clark/Wolverhampton Library*

Below:
Much of Wolverhampton High Level's beauty was hidden away in quiet corners, such as this canopy detail dating from the rebuilding of the station in 1884, and recorded for posterity in June 1960.
J. H. Denton/W. K. V. Gale, courtesy Wolverhampton Library

January 1962 as part of the Euston-Crewe electrification scheme.

Bushbury Shed

Freed from having to share the High Level station with the GWR, the LNWR set about improving some of its facilities there. As we have seen, little thought was given to the passengers, but some attention was paid to housing the motive power. The original LNWR Wolverhampton engine shed was built with the station in 1852 and was situated about 350yd due north of it. By 1859 it was far too small for its allocation, and a site for a new larger shed was chosen at Bushbury, 1½ miles north of Wolverhampton, just beyond Bushbury Junction and station, where the company's Stour Valley and Grand Junction lines met. This timber-built shed held a dozen locomotives under cover. The former shed was converted for use as a carriage shed, and, with extensions added in 1889, was used as such

until the High Level station was redeveloped in the mid-1960s. As Bushbury developed as a stabling point for locomotives on both local services and the LNWR's crack Birmingham-London expresses, within 20 years its allocation had grown to over 40 engines. In January 1877 for example, 'Bloomers' Nos 996 *Raglan*, 998 *Una*, 999 *Medusa*, 1000 *Umpire* and 1002 *Theseus* were noted there for working trains between London and Crewe.

Once more, a new shed was needed; so a larger brick shed was constructed on the site of the timber one at Bushbury in 1883. This had eight roads, and was originally provided with only one turntable of 42ft replaced by a 50ft one in 1905 to handle larger locomotives on the accelerated services to Euston. With some modifications, this was the shed which served Wolverhampton's 'North Western' lines until the 1960s. It used local coal and drew water from its own well. A second turntable was added by the end of the LNWR days, and was relocated by the LMS,

Above:
A romantic prewar view of Bushbury shed in LMS days. The range of buildings on the extreme left were the works of the Star Motor Co. *Eric Hamilton Collection*

which also added a 70ft turntable and mechanised the coaling and ash disposal processes.

Bushbury's allocation reached almost 60 engines in the mid-1920s declining to around 40 over the

Below:
The victor and the vanquished. D378 (40178) on the 10.05am Glasgow-Birmingham service passing Bushbury shed on 4 August 1962. Note the mechanised coaling apparatus competing with the signals for dominance of the skyline; and the bicycle rack!
Michael Mensing

next 30 years. For many years shunting in the shed yard, and in and around Wolverhampton, was the duty of older classes of locomotive; veteran '2F' 0-6-0s Nos 8216, 8230, 8234 and 28209 sharing the task with 0-6-0Ts Nos 7396-7399 and Nos 7413 and 7473. By 1940, Euston trains were in the charge of 'Royal Scots' which had replaced the 'Jubilees', with only No 5734 left to run some slower services.

Diesel power, in the form of two shunters, was first allocated to Bushbury in 1954; these were part of the order for 573 such locomotives placed by BR in December 1951. Also in 1954, Bushbury's allocation of eight Class 6 locomotives sometimes proved inadequate to cover its five daily London duties, one of which lasted over 24hr therefore requiring six locomotives in steam each day; but with the start of that year's winter timetable, certain of Camden shed's duties were switched to Bushbury, which had its allocation slightly increased as well.

This was the last time on which the shed's steam locomotive allocation was increased, and despite the opening of a new BR social club adjacent to the shed in the autumn of 1956, increasing numbers of diesels heralded its end as an operating depot. Finally within this period, Bushbury shed was renumbered 21C in 1960, having been 3B under the LMS and BR before, and 13 under the LNWR.

The Wolverhampton & Walsall Railway

Completing Wolverhampton's 'North Western' lines was the Wolverhampton & Walsall Railway (W&WR). This was authorised by an Act of 29 June 1865 to construct a 6-mile line between a junction with the GWR at Wolverhampton and the South Staffordshire Railway at Ryecroft Junction, just north of Walsall. A supplementary Act of 23 July 1866 transferred the Wolverhampton junction of the line to one with the Stour Valley line of the LNWR, involving construction of an additional 3/4-mile of line; the latter company also being granted running powers over it when completed. A further Act of 12 August 1867 extended the time allowed to build the line until 12 August 1870, and granted the Midland Railway running powers over the South Staffordshire lines of the LNWR and over its lines between Bescot and Wolverhampton, which it first exercised on 1 September that year. A final Act of 20 June 1870 extended the construction period until 1 December 1872; it just ducking in under the tape and opening on 1 November 1872.

Nominally independent, the W&WR was worked jointly by the LNWR and Midland companies and had stations at Heath Town, Wednesfield, Willenhall (Market Place), Short Heath, Bentley and North Walsall. After three years of operation under an agreement requiring each company to send all traffic between Wolverhampton and Walsall via the line, together with any traffic for which it formed the shortest route, disagreement arose between the LNWR and the Midland over the interpretation of this agreement that resulted in legal proceedings.

Basically, the LNWR owned alternate routes over which it had been sending much of the goods traffic that should have gone via the W&WR. Arbitration won the day again, but the LNWR made an offer to purchase the line, partly to end the need for the meticulous bookkeeping that joint operation of it necessitated, and partly because it knew that the Midland would like to buy it once another line in which it was interested, the Wolverhampton Walsall & Midland Junction line (WW&MJ), was completed. This extended the W&WR from both North Walsall and Walsall stations, via Sutton Coldfield, to a junction with the Midland Railway near Castle Bromwich; and offered the Midland a direct route from its traditional heartland to Wolverhampton and possibly (as we shall see in Chapter 6) beyond to South Wales.

The W&WR was vested in the LNWR from 1 July 1875, which sold it to the Midland on 1 July 1876, the latter retaining running powers into the High Level station until 30 June 1878; LNWR services over the W&WR ending on 31 July 1876. Thus facing the loss of its base in Wolverhampton, the Midland planned to build its own station there, on a site on the Wednesfield Road further below the GWR's Low Level station, as detailed in the Midland (New Works &c) Act passed on 28 June 1877.

That same day the LNWR obtained two sets of further powers. The first was to construct the Wolverhampton Junction Railway, a 1¼-mile link line between the W&WR at Heath Town and its Grand Junction line on the site of Portobello station (closed on 1 January 1873). This, with additional curves at Walsall, would allow the LNWR to resume more direct through working between Wolverhampton and Walsall. The second was to extend the High Level station, which brought opposition from the GWR and Midland companies, which complained this would spoil access to their stations. Matters were resolved by a House of Commons Select Committee, which restricted the spread of the High Level station and renegotiated the Midland's right to use it. Thus stuck with permission to build a passenger station, and no need to do so, the Midland decided to build a goods station there instead; construction of Wednesfield Road goods station taking three years, between November 1878 and November 1881.

And so Wolverhampton's 'North Western' lines were complete; the by now Midland-owned WW&MJ line having opened on 1 July 1879 and the LNWR's Wolverhampton Junction line on 1 March 1881.

The Development of Passenger Services

The complex pattern of 'North Western' lines that was developed in the Wolverhampton area allowed no fewer than five alternate routes between the town and Birmingham: four LNWR and one Midland, with a corresponding degree of flexibility in the operation of train services, particularly local ones, between them.

Below:
Midland Railway '3F' 0-6-0 No 3787 stands in front of Wednesfield Road Goods station with a Lysaght train.
Bennett Clark, via J. Hughes

L. & N. W. R.

CLOSING OF PASSENGER STATIONS

NOTICE IS HEREBY GIVEN that, on and from 1st JANUARY, 1917, the following Passenger Stations and Halts will be closed until further notice:—

ASPLEY GUISE HALT	KEMPSTON AND	PLECK
BATH ROAD HALT	ELSTOW HALT	PONT RUG
BOW BRICKHILL HALT	KEMPSTON HARDWICK HALT	PORT MEADOW HALT
CARPENDERS PARK	KILBURN & MAIDA VALE	QUEEN'S PARK (BILINGTON)
CARR MILL	LLONG	RHOSNEIGR
CHALK FARM	LOUDOUN ROAD	RUGBY ROAD HALT
CHARLTON HALT	LOWTON	SANKEY BRIDGES
CHEADLE	MAIDEN LANE	STAINCLIFFE & BATLEY CARR
CHURCH BRAMPTON	MOCHDRE & PABO	STAR CROSSING HALT
CHURWELL	MONMORE GREEN	UPPERMILL
FRIEZLAND	MOORE	WENDLEBURY HALT
HALEBANK	NANTLLE	WOLVERCOTE HALT
HAMMERSMITH & CHISWICK	ODDINGTON HALT	WOODSTOCK ROAD HALT
HOOLEY HILL	OVER & WHARTON	WOOTTON BROADMEAD HALT
HUSBORNE CRAWLEY HALT	OXFORD ROAD HALT	WOOTTON PILLINGE HALT

GUY CALTHROP. *General Manager*

Above:
Many halts and stations were temporarily closed during World War 1 due to staff shortages. Some reopened afterwards, but this notice spelled the end for Monmore Green. *Railway Gazette*

1 – Local passenger services

Local LNWR passenger services continued to use Wednesfield Heath station until September 1853, when it was closed; reopening between 1 August 1855 and 1 January 1873, when it finally closed to passengers, along with Portobello station, and the section of the GJR line between Bushbury and Willenhall to regular passenger trains. From the opening of the South Staffordshire Railway in November 1847, this had provided a somewhat tortuous link to Walsall, requiring reversals at Bushbury and Bescot junctions, but was superseded when the Wolverhampton & Walsall line opened.

For some years, a service of four connecting trains at Walsall maintained a local Birmingham service along the GJR line, but this was less important after the Stour Valley line opened a more direct route which, from opening, had a daily service of 10 trains each way. The journey took 50min, but included a 10-15min ticket collection stop at Edgbaston (Monument Lane) station; something that was possibly suspended when a service every ½hr was introduced on the Stour Valley line between 1 May 1853 and 1 July 1854 so that the LNWR could claim the line was too busy to allow S&B trains to use it.

North of Wolverhampton, a station was opened at Bushbury Junction on 2 August 1852, as a ticket collection point for the High Level; but this was not served by the four daily extended workings of Stour Valley trains that called at the local stations to Stafford — Four Ashes, Spread Eagle (Gailey after 1 August 1881), and Penkridge. Wolverhampton-Stafford local services gradually increased in number over the next century or so, with only the closure of two of the intermediate stations, Gailey (18 June 1951), and Four Ashes (15 June 1959), to mar this improvement.

The opening of the Wolverhampton Junction link line, between Heath Town and Portobello, and the Pleck curve, saw the beginning of a greater diversity in local passenger services. Before the Grouping, Midland trains to Birmingham along the WW&MJ line from Walsall were worked over these via the GJR line to Walsall to avoid the need for reversal; whereas LNWR local services to Walsall, which had to reverse there, were run along the Midland-owned W&W line. Thus, for 40 years or so, the latter's Midland stations were served daily by an average of nine LNWR trains and only one Midland train.

A final variation in local Wolverhampton services began on 1 April 1889 with the opening of the Soho loop line, which connected the GJR and Stour Valley lines about two miles out of Birmingham. Trains bound for New Street, along either of these lines, could now enter the station from either its north (Stour Valley), or south (L&B) ends; but from Wolverhampton it was used by four afternoon LNWR/GJR line Birmingham trains to eliminate the need for locomotive run-rounds in New Street station at busy periods.

There were a few station closures in the Wolverhampton area in the first decades of this century, but these made little difference to the basic train services. Bushbury, a small wooden station with low, exposed platforms, was closed on 1 May 1912; its role as a ticket collection point having gone in 1910. It only took £42 in 1911. Monmore Green, the first station on the Stour Valley line out of the town, closed temporarily on 1 January 1917 due to wartime staff shortages, but did not reopen after the war, and its closure was made permanent from December 1920. Finally, North Walsall, a station on the W&WR line, closed on 13 July 1925.

After the Grouping, all of Wolverhampton's 'North Western' lines came under LMS control, and operational anomalies, such as the working of the W&WR line mentioned above, were rationalised;

Above:
The introduction of DMUs on to Wolverhampton's 'North Western' lines enabled a number of services to be revised and extended, such as Walsall trains running through to Burton-on-Trent. Here an empty DMU enters the High Level past No 3 signalbox. *R. C. Riley*

and for a brief period local services flourished. A 1926 LMS working timetable for the Wolverhampton area reveals the following number of services operating daily: to Stafford, five, plus one Motor Train; to Birmingham (Stour Valley line), 16; to Birmingham (GJR line to Walsall, then WW&MJ), one; to Vauxhall (GJR line), one; to Walsall (GJR line), 12 plus two Motor Trains; to Derby (via GJR line to Walsall and South Staffs line), one; to Walsall (Midland W&W line), five, plus one Motor Train; to Bescot via Walsall, three, plus two Motor Trains; to Bescot (GJR line direct), one, plus one Motor Train, plus extended Stour Valley line workings to Coventry (one) and Rugby (one).

From 1930 onwards the LMS cut back on loss-making local services in the West Midlands; the W&W line closing to passengers from 5 January 1931 as a consequence of this policy. Also the Soho loop line was closed to passengers from 5 May 1941. By 1947, on the eve of railway nationalisation, Wolverhampton's local LMS services consisted of 18 Stour Valley line trains, five of which were semi-fasts, the majority of the remainder also calling at local stations from Stafford; seven peak hours-only GJR line Birmingham trains, travelling via Walsall, plus three short workings to Walsall only. Trains had ceased going to Birmingham via the WW&MJ line, this in 1947 being used only by Walsall-Birmingham services. Certain local passenger services in the Birmingham area of British Railways (London Midland Region) were taken over by diesel multiple-units (DMUs) on 1 March 1956, but these did not come into widespread use in the Wolverhampton area until November 1958, when they were introduced on local services to Stafford and on those working through Walsall. Albion

station, on the Stour Valley line, closed to passengers on 2 February 1960; but otherwise, by 1962, services on this line and to Stafford from Wolverhampton were maintained at 14 and 16 trains daily, respectively. Twelve Walsall trains also remained, nine of which, with the wider introduction of DMUs in November 1958, had been extended through to Burton-on-Trent via the South Staffs line through Pelsall, one of which ran an evening short-working to Lichfield along the same route.

2 — Express passenger services

From the opening of the LNWR's Trent Valley line on 1 December 1847, the company had an alternate route for its crack northern expresses which avoided the operational slack that resulted when trains threaded their way through the tangle of lines around Birmingham and Wolverhampton. From this date Wolverhampton would seem to have been condemned to performing a secondary role with regard to LNWR expresses. Yet, within a short time following the opening of the High Level station, it was to become the northern base of that company's premier Birmingham-London expresses.

In 1841, a journey from Euston to Wolverhampton via the L&B and GJR lines was not one to be undertaken lightly. Third-class, by the slowest trains, took 8hr 20min, including a 1¾hr wait at Birmingham; first-class, by the fastest trains, a mere

5½hr, with only a 15min wait at Birmingham. By 1855, with a united railway, and new lines and stations at Birmingham and Wolverhampton, only 20min had been lopped off the third-class journey time, whilst first-class passengers could now travel the distance in 4hr 10min flat.

A number of factors contributed towards the acceleration of the LNWR's Wolverhampton-London expresses. By May 1859, the elimination of refreshment stops and calls at the majority of the intermediate stations had reduced the time to Birmingham to 3hr. A less obvious factor was the creation of the LNWR's Central District in 1860. This ran from Rugby to Stafford, embracing all of the company's lines around Birmingham and Wolverhampton; the District Superintendent being responsible for all operational matters within this area. Within a short time of this, the newly-opened Bushbury shed became the northern operating base for the Euston expresses (the southern base being Camden shed), which, by starting from Wolverhampton, gained both many additional passengers and a useful stabling point away from the bustle of New Street and Monument Lane.

To counter this, the 12¾ miles of the Stour Valley line, with its dozen stations and saw-tooth gradients, offered little opportunity for speed; being generally disliked by most drivers, who, in more polite moments, described it as a 'Fred Karno's backyard'. A remedy for this came on 1 March 1882 with the opening of a line linking Stechford, on the L&B line, with Aston, on the GJR line. This enabled expresses to be divided at Stechford, the front portion going fast to Wolverhampton via the GJR line and Portobello Junction, the rear portion continuing on to New Street and working to Wolverhampton as a stopping service along the Stour Valley line.

Further acceleration of the Wolverhampton-London expresses came mainly through locomotive developments. Eventually, on 1 March 1905, a service of three daily expresses that could cover the journey between Birmingham and London in 2hr, nonstop, was introduced. This spurred the GWR into investing heavily in shortening its route between London and Birmingham and the LNWR into accelerating its service still further. As the opening of the new GWR route approached in 1910, the LNWR ran a number of accelerated trips between Euston and Birmingham New Street, one run on 28 November 1909 achieving an impressive 1hr 51min, hauled by 4-4-0 'Precursor' No 1387 *Lang Meg*.

Another well established way of competing for passengers between London and Birmingham was through the standard of service they were offered. With an eye to the prestigious business traveller, on 1 February 1910 the LNWR inaugurated its 'City to City' expresses between Wolverhampton and London (Broad Street), then the company's only named express. It was formed by four specially constructed large bogie coaches, those at each end being corridor compartment cars. In between were a first, a second and a third-class dining and refreshment car, on which breakfast and dinner could be taken, and one of the compartments had

Below:
A two-car Gloucester DMU approaches Wolverhampton High Level with the 4.44pm Lichfield — Burton–on–Trent service which enjoyed a brief period of rejuvenation with the introduction of DMUs. Unfortunately this was too little, too late and the service was withdrawn in 1965. Note the 3C (Walsall Ryecroft) shed code, the paraphernalia of steam, and the permanent way hut which is on the site later to be occupied by Wolverhampton power signalbox.
Michael Mensing

Top:
The familiar scene at Wolverhampton High Level after 2 November 1959 when London expresses were abolished for four years pending work on electrification. A Gloucester-built two-car DMU stands on the left with two Park Royal units on the right.
A. J. Wheeler

Above:
LMS 'Rebuilt Scot' class 4-6-0 No 46111 *Royal Fusilier* hauls a nine-coach train up the 1 in 94 bank between Tipton and Deepfields stations with the 10.30am Euston to Wolverhampton service on Sunday 30 July 1961. The 'GWR' line crosses in the background, to the rear of the elevated Bloomfield Junction signalbox.
Michael Mensing

The Development of Goods Facilities and Services

The Wolverhampton District was one in which the LNWR did a very heavy mineral business, including, as it did, the numerous blast furnaces and ironworks in South Staffordshire, and also the Cannock Chase coalfield, plus the many manufacturers of the town itself. The original LNWR goods station and warehouses were those of the former Grand Junction company at Wednesfield Heath, illustrated earlier, which were its sole goods facilities in Wolverhampton until late September 1859, following purchase of the GWR's S&B half share in the High Level station. On this site there was a purpose-built goods station, with access from Old Mill Street and Corn Hill, but known as Mill Street Goods. This included four warehouses and its own integral canal basins with four loading faces.

The early 1860s were an important period in the establishment of Wolverhampton's 'North Western' lines goods operations. Firstly, the formation of the LNWR's Central District, mentioned above, also meant changes in its goods department. With Birmingham seen as too remote from the area's industry, Wolverhampton was chosen as the head-quarters of the LNWR's South Staffordshire and East Worcestershire Goods District. This needed accommodation, and the former S&B company offices, over the arched entrance to the High Level station, were selected as the most suitable. Temporarily let out as an auction room, these were reacquired and began operation in October 1860 as the offices of the Wolverhampton District Goods Manager.

Secondly, a network of colliery lines was acquired that gained the LNWR access to the Cannock Chase coalfields. The South Staffordshire Railway had opened a branch line from Walsall to Cannock on 1 February 1858, which the LNWR acquired when it took that company over exactly three years later. Leaving this line at Hednesford was the Cannock Chase Railway, built by the landowner, the Marquis of Anglesey, to his collieries there; and authorised on 15 May 1860, with an extension authorised on 29 July 1862. The LNWR acquired this on 28 July

1863. Joining these lines later, under the LMS, was a Midland Railway branch from Aldridge, on the WW&MJ line, to Brownhills through the Walsall Wood Collieries, which was opened on 1 July 1884; the Midland Railway having, three years earlier, also opened its goods station on the Wednesfield Road.

Credit for the development of the LNWR Wolverhampton Goods District rests with two men, Thomas Mitchellhill (1857-1912) and Walter Ree. Mitchellhill was appointed District Goods Manager there on 1 February 1887, remaining until 31 December 1908, during which time he built up a considerable mineral traffic and encouraged the laying of many private sidings. On 10 September 1902, the LNWR began operating from the canal basin of the Chillington ironworks tramway, adjacent to its Monmore Green station, having built a loop from its Stour Valley line to gain access to it. This had been planned from March 1897, the basin becoming known as Monmore Green Goods. Mitchellhill left to become the Mineral Traffic Manager of the whole LNWR system and was succeeded by Walter Ree, who restructured the District Goods Manager's Office, installing a Canvassing Department to actively seek business. Ree left in August 1911, eventually rising to become Goods Operating Manager for the whole of the LMS.

Ree's aggressive marketing tactics paid off. With the rising threat from road transport in the late 1920s, the Wolverhampton Goods District adopted the slogan: 'To wrest from the road the traffic that sustains us', which it did very successfully. By 1937 it served some 750 square miles: from Soho in Birmingham to Penkridge, embracing Wellington and Coalport, Stourport-on-Severn, Cannock Chase and Lichfield, an area containing 750,000 people. Seventy staff co-ordinated 51 goods depots and 200 private sidings, employing 300 horses and 200 motor

Below:
The scene immediately behind the Wolverhampton District Goods Manager's Office (DGMO) at the High Level station around 1910. The cart is standing on the former station carriage drive, which was diverted in 1883. *Wolverhampton Library*

vehicles for cartage and deliveries. In 1936, the District transported 5,060,459 tons of coal and 3,604,576 tons of minerals and merchandise.

The Wolverhampton Goods District continued into British Railways days, until, under a £5.5 million Midland Freight Traffic Plan, announced on 20 January 1959, it closed on 28 April 1960, five months short of its centenary, leaving operations at Mill Street, Wednesfield Road and Monmore Green to be run from Birmingham.

Above:
Despite its ramshackle appearance, Wednesfield Road Goods station has remained open. This view shows the main vehicular entrance off the Wednesfield Road. *Keith Hodgkins*

Below:
The goods avoiding lines at Wolverhampton High Level are shown to good effect in this shot of ex-GWR 0-6-0PT No 9798 working an assortment of goods wagons past the station in the early 1960s. *Lionel J. Lee*

3: The Great Western Lines to 1962

Although the Great Western Railway (GWR) was commenced primarily to connect Bristol with London, the success of the country's first main trunk railways, the London & Birmingham and Grand Junction lines, ensured that extensions towards the north were very soon taken in hand. Whilst these extensions were projected as more or less independent railways, the GWR took an active interest in their construction, acquiring most of them before they were completed. The GWR also championed its Engineer's own broad gauge, the use of which gave it an exclusivity of access to certain regions; the spread of which was bitterly opposed by those railway companies operating upon the standard or 'narrow' gauge. Conflict was inevitable, and it was resolved by the establishment of a Royal Commission which was directed to consider the benefit to the nation of the adoption of a uniform gauge.

The Gauge Commission

The Gauge Commission was set up on 9 July 1845, and sat for 30 days between 6 August and 18 December that year. It heard witnesses and conducted experiments, publishing a report on 17 February 1846 which recommended that: 'the gauge of 4ft 8½in be declared to be the gauge to be used in all public Railways now under construction or hereafter to be constructed in Great Britain'. This became the basis of the Regulation of Gauges Act, which, swayed by powerful lobbying and the sheer length of lines either open or approved using the standard gauge (biased roughly 5:1) received the Royal Assent on 18 August 1846. It prohibited the future construction of any passenger railway in Great Britain at any other gauge.

In fact this was far from the end of the matter. The Act went on to exempt from this dictum any future railway Act containing a special enactment defining its line's gauge or gauges. Put simply, anyone promoting a non-standard gauge railway could build it, if they could prove the need to use the gauge they specified. Nonetheless, history shows that the only broad gauge lines sanctioned by Parliament *after* 1846 were short branches or extensions to lines it had authorised *before* then.

The Oxford Railway

The map in the original GWR prospectus of 1833 showed a branch to Oxford, but efforts to build this were thwarted until the successful promotion of the Oxford Railway Company in 1842. By an Act of 11 April 1843, this company was authorised to build a 10-mile branch from the GWR main line at Didcot to Oxford, which it did; the line opening on 12 June 1844, 33 days after it had been amalgamated with the GWR. Although seemingly remote, this line was already common to the proposals of two railway

Below:
How the GWR saw Wolverhampton. A page from its Through the Window – Paddington to Birkenhead book published in 1925. Notice the emphasis given to 'other lines' and the importance accredited to Codsall!
Author's Collection

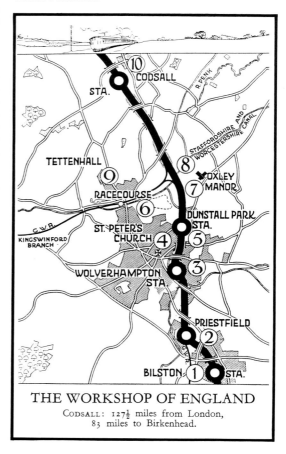

THE WORKSHOP OF ENGLAND
CODSALL: 127½ miles from London,
83 miles to Birkenhead.

companies through which the GWR would eventually reach Wolverhampton.

The Oxford, Worcester & Wolverhampton Railway

In August 1836, the GWR Directors considered the continuation of their proposed Oxford branch to Worcester, to link up with a line then being promoted between there and Wolverhampton: The Grand Connection Railway (see Chapter 6). The latter was not built, but, eight years later, the preliminary work done for this line, notably surveys of expected goods traffic, were to prove invaluable to a scheme incorporating both of these earlier proposals.

Once a line striking north from the GWR's main line between Bristol and London had been opened, however short, the impetus was given for the promotion of lines to continue this further north. The Oxford & Rugby Railway scheme was adopted by the GWR in the spring of 1844. Rugby was a junction between the L&B and Midland Counties lines, and thus afforded access to both the Northwest, via the GJR, and to Derbyshire and Yorkshire. It was to be built on the broad gauge.

The Oxford Worcester & Wolverhampton Railway (OWW) was promoted in August 1844 by a consortium of local businessmen in the towns along its proposed route which ran from a branch off the GJR at its Wolverhampton station, via Dudley, Stourbridge, Kidderminster, Droitwich, Worcester, Pershore and Evesham, to a junction with the planned Oxford & Rugby Railway a few miles north of Banbury. Its prospectus also noted that the GWR had agreed to guarantee an annual payment of 3½% on the total estimated capital for the line; something confirmed in a formal agreement between the two companies, signed on 20 September 1844, which also moved the junction with the Oxford & Rugby line much nearer Oxford.

This guarantee, together with a well produced prospectus, should have secured the OWW Bill an easy passage through Parliament, but the Royal Assent it gained on 4 August 1845 was hard fought. The Bill contained powers to lease or sell the OWW to the GWR, which was also empowered to complete the line if the OWW failed to, or if called upon by the Board of Trade to do so; thus inheriting the OWW's powers over the line. It was to be broad gauge throughout, a point which unleashed a torrent of opposition to the Bill, not the least of which came

Below:
'51XX' class No 4104 takes a Stourbridge to Wolverhampton local train past Daisy Bank & Bradley station on 30 July 1961 exactly a year before the passenger service along this line was withdrawn.
Michael Mensing

Above:
Modified 'Hall' No 7904 *Fountains Hall* works a return excursion from Malvern Wells through Princes End and Coseley station on Whit Monday 11 June 1962, showing the spartan nature of the station's facilities. Local passenger services along the line were withdrawn just seven weeks later. *Michael Mensing*

The OWW became known as the 'Old Worse & Worse' which was not surprising really, because that was just how things got. On 1 June 1849 the OWW's Directors reported that practically all the money was spent and there was not a mile of workable line to show for it. This was underlined by a Railway Commission inspection of the route by Capt Simmons on 27 November 1849, his report of which ends: 'At each end of the line a great deal of work remains to be done, but from Evesham by Worcester and Stourbridge to near Dudley the works are very far advanced and nearly ready for opening, with the exception of stations and the permanent way not being laid'. This report was part of an attempt by the Board of Trade to persuade the GWR to comply with the terms of the OWW Act and intervene to complete the line. It declined; was ordered to act, refused, and was taken to court, the lengthy proceedings that ensued being dropped on 28 April 1851 because the OWW was by then completing the work itself.

The route opened to passenger services in nine stages: Abbotswood Junction (with Midland Railway) to Worcester (5 October 1850); Worcester to Droitwich and branch to Stoke Prior (18 February 1852); Worcester to Evesham (1 May 1852); Droitwich to Stourbridge (3 May 1852); Stourbridge to Dudley (20 December 1852); Evesham to Oxford (4 June 1853); Dudley to Tipton, plus a standard gauge connection with the LNWR's Stour Valley line at Tipton — the Tipton Curve (1 December 1853) — and both Tipton to Priestfield, to a junction with the GWR, and Cannock Road Junction to Bushbury (1 July 1854).

All but the final section had at least one broad gauge rail laid upon it, although the only recorded use made of this was the running of two inspection trains; the first of these travelling between Oxford and Evesham on 2 June 1853, a second train running between Wolverhampton and Harborough, and Evesham and Honeybourne, on 17 November 1853. In his report on the latter inspection, the redoubtable Capt Galton reported that he had inspected the mixed gauge line and could pass it all for use as a double line of narrow gauge and a single line of mixed gauge, except for the 5-mile section between Evesham and Honeybourne, the opening of which 'would be attended with danger to the public from the incompleteness of the permanent way'.

Between Tipton and Wolverhampton there were stations at Daisey Bank (Daisy Bank from February 1866 and Daisy Bank & Bradley from 5 May 1919), Bilston (Bilston West from 19 July 1950), and Priestfield; with an additional station opened at Princes End, before Daisey Bank, in December 1856, which became Princes End & Coseley from 6 January 1936.

In April 1852, C. C. Williams of London, a locomotive contractor, was engaged to work the 36

from the L&B and Midland companies. The furore which followed precipitated the Gauge Commission referred to above, and set the pattern for the line's first 10 years.

The OWW was engineered by I. K. Brunel himself, who had to revise his estimate of the line's cost from £1½ million to £2½ million to take account of extra works required, conditional upon the passing of the company's Bill. Already undersubscribed, the GWR agreed to increase its guarantee to 4%pa on the revised capital estimate of £2½ million. This began a 10-year period of intense ill-feeling between the OWW and GWR Boards; much of which does not concern railways, or Wolverhampton, and takes McDermot 37 pages to detail. It is the story of the OWW's autocratic Chairmen and Directors; their imprudent financial dealings, deception of the shareholders, and attempts to lease the line to other companies, familiar stuff in the period of railway mania. Its relevance here is not in what was done, but in what was not done; ie the building of a railway to Wolverhampton.

miles of the OWW to be opened by 1 May of that year. Williams appointed David Joy, of valve gear fame, as his Locomotive Superintendent; Joy being sent off to scour the country for suitable locomotives. He found four: 'Went to Welwyn — Great Northern Railway — and got *Mudlark*, a contractor's engine; to Offord — got a big six-coupled long boiler . . . . Then to Shrewsbury to hire Shrewsbury & Hereford engines; had to see Jeffreys [Locomotive Superintendent of the Shrewsbury & Hereford Railway] before breakfast, but he could spare none. On to Leeds and Pontefract after a four-coupled *Jenny*, a contractor's engine, just put in fine order at Railway Foundry . . . . Then to Leeds to see a little engine in the shops at Railway Foundry — called *Canary*, she was a little mite. Arranged for all of these to go to Worcester.' In November 1852, the OWW took delivery of the first of its own locomotives, and by August 1855 had built up quite an impressive rolling stock, as shown in Appendix 2. Williams' contract ended on 1 February 1856; Joy being retained as Locomotive Superintendent for a few months.

Top:
GWR No 279 was originally OWW No 33 built by E. B. Wilson & Co in 1855 to work ballast trains. It is seen here in the early 1870s in original condition, in which it remained until withdrawal in August 1885. *LPC*

Above:
GWR No 291 was WM No 97, a tender goods engine built in 1861 by W. Fairbairn & Sons to a design by Kirtley of the Midland Railway. Like No 279, it was not rebuilt, and remained in original and, when photographed around 1880, quite tatty condition until withdrawal in April 1882. *LPC*

Joy left just as the OWW's fortunes took a turn for the better. A new Board was appointed in June 1856, the quarrelsome element retiring; the important job of General Manager being given to A. C. Sherriff, late of the North Eastern Railway, who so took to Worcester that he stayed there, becoming a councillor and the city's MP. Operating losses declined, and by February 1858 the company was talking to the GWR again. On 1 March 1858 a new accord came into force, confirming an OWW/GWR traffic agreement; the GWR agreeing to remove broad gauge rails south of Priestfield.

The West Midland Railway

A scheme to build a railway joining Worcester and Hereford was incorporated on 15 August 1853, but was in danger of lapsing for want of capital when it was taken up by the Newport Abergavenny & Hereford Railway (NA&H) as forming a valuable link between its line and the OWW. A further Act of August 1858 established funding for the line jointly with the OWW and Midland companies; and by the time the first section of the new line opened in July 1859, the OWW and NA&H saw the sense in amalgamating all three lines into one company. An Act to this effect was passed on 14 June 1860, the new West Midland Railway (WM) taking effect from 1 July.

Wags, mindful of the OWW's old nickname, soon christened this the 'Werry Middlin' ', but for once this was unfair. The new company retained A. C. Sherriff as General Manager and became an active promoter of six continuation lines: The Severn Valley Railway, The Witney Railway, The Bourton-on-the-Water Railway, The Much Wenlock & Severn Junction Railway, The Tenbury & Bewdley Railway and the Stourbridge Railway. Through the abortive promotion of a further line at the start of 1861, discussions began with the GWR, resulting in two agreements: one, on 4 May, for the latter to lease the OWW section of the WM; another, on 30 May, for the two companies to amalgamate. The leasing arrangement began on 1 June 1861, managed by a joint committee, the amalgamation being sanctioned by an Act of 13 July 1863, and effective from 1 August; the new company having 18 GWR Directors and six from the WM, adding a further 281 miles of standard gauge and 2 miles of mixed gauge to the former.

The Birmingham Wolverhampton & Dudley Railway

On paper, the GWR's other approach to Wolverhampton may seem even more convoluted than that via the OWW, being made up, as it was, of three separate schemes. But this was not so. From the common root of the Oxford Railway, the Oxford & Rugby Railway (O&R), already mentioned, was promoted at a public meeting in Oxford on 14 May 1844, attended by several GWR luminaries, including Brunel. The route does not appear to have been finalised at this stage, as, under questioning, Brunel was of the opinion that it should run to Birmingham; but the 'Rugby' camp won the day, an Act being obtained on 4 August 1845. Work commenced soon afterwards, the company amalgamating with the GWR on 14 May 1846. The broad gauge O&R line opened to Banbury on 2 September 1850, and to

Fenny Compton on 1 October 1852 the intention of proceeding to Rugby having been dropped in 1849.

The next scheme, advancing the GWR towards Wolverhampton by this route, was born of the keen rivalry between the L&B and GJR companies. In 1845, the latter promoted a line from its Birmingham terminus, via Warwick and Leamington, to join the GWR at Oxford, and thus gain independent access to London. This was the Birmingham & Oxford Junction Railway (B&O). In Parliament, opposition to the scheme was fierce, and it was thrown out. Undaunted, a meeting of the intended shareholders was held in Birmingham on 13 May 1845, who resolved to resubmit a Bill to Parliament together with one extending the line to a new station site in Birmingham, to be built on the plot of land described by Monmouth Street and Great Charles Street, and Livery Street and Snow Hill.

At the same meeting, the advisability of extending the line on through to Dudley was discussed; leading to the establishment of a further scheme to take the line on to Wolverhampton. Called the Birmingham Wolverhampton & Dudley Railway (BW&D), this was nominally independent, but essentially the work of the same promoters as the B&O line. Both schemes presented Bills before Parliament in 1846, gaining the Royal Assent on the same day, 3 August 1846. To avoid trouble, each had omitted to specify the gauge to which they would be built, and so by the Regulation of Gauges Act passed just 15 days later they were, by default, to be narrow gauge.

At the first shareholders' meetings of the B&O and BW&D, both held on 30 October 1846, resolutions were passed, under mutual powers contained in each other's Acts, to amalgamate the two companies, and to sell or lease this new company to the GWR. On 12 November 1846, the GWR agreed to buy the companies, the Boards of all them meeting to confirm this arrangement on 4 December. This was duly done by the GWR and BW&D Boards, but the B&O faced opposition in the form of a rival offer from the LNWR to buy its line, only at a much higher price than the GWR was offering. Many 'dirty deeds' were done in trying to close this deal, the GWR having to resort to legal action to compel the B&O's compliance with its prior agreement. It took a High Court ruling on 4 December 1847 which had been a wasted year to obtain this. The BW&D and B&O companies had not been amalgamated and vested in the GWR before an Act gaining the Royal Assent on 31 August 1848; which also allowed the GWR to lay mixed gauge track on the B&O and BW&D lines.

Construction on the BW&D began in 1851 and the B&O opened to passengers on 1 October 1852, the same day as the Banbury-Fenny Compton section of the O&R; the BW&D eventually opening to Priestfield on 14 November 1854, having been delayed by the collapse of a bridge over a road between Soho and Handsworth stations on 26 August, the day *after*

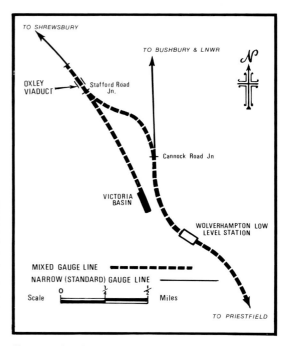

it had passed a Board of Trade inspection. At Priestfield, the BW&D joined the OWW, which had been compelled by Parliament to complete its mixed gauge line from there into Wolverhampton. On the BW&D, there were stations between Wednesbury and Wolverhampton, at Wednesbury (Wednesbury Central from 1 July 1950), Bilston (Bilston Central from 1 July 1950) and Priestfield, with an additional station opened at Bradley & Moxley, after Wednesbury, in June 1860.

The Shrewsbury & Birmingham Railway and the Limit of the Broad Gauge

It was noted in the previous chapter that the S&B Railway was amalgamated with the GWR on 1 September 1854, being delayed in commencing services from the GWR/OWW Wolverhampton Joint station for the same reason as the BW&D. By way of preparation for this, the GWR had obtained powers under an Act of 30 June 1852 to construct the ¾-mile Wolverhampton Junction Railway, a mixed gauge

line running between Cannock Road Junction, the northern extremity of the OWW's mixed gauge, and Stafford Road Junction, where the narrow gauge S&B line joined. Two years later the GWR also obtained powers to convert about a mile of the S&B to mixed gauge, from Stafford Road Junction into the S&B's Victoria Canal basin, plus sidings there, and on into its Stafford Road locomotive repair shops (see Chapter 4). These lines also came into use on 14 November 1854, and were the most northerly point reached by the GWR's broad gauge.

Above:

Wednesbury was one of the original stations opening with the BW&D on 14 November 1854. It is seen here on 28 May 1960, when it was called Wednesbury Central, with a DMU on a Wellington to Leamington Spa working. *R. C. Riley*

Below:

Wolverhampton Joint station in 1856. *Ian Allan Library*

The Low Level station

Wolverhampton's Great Western station was planned as part of the OWW line. Under an Act of 14 August 1848, this was to be constructed and maintained jointly with and for the use of the BW&D and S&B companies; from which it became known, initially, as the Wolverhampton 'Joint' station. Appropriately, it was also designed jointly, with the buildings being the work of John Fowler, the trackwork by Henry Robertson and overall roof by Brunel. Indeed, this was to be the great engineer's last work on a railway station, and the last of his 'one-sided' stations to be built.

Construction of the station overran its opening, with the completion of the OWW line from Priestfield, on 1 July 1854. The station was still

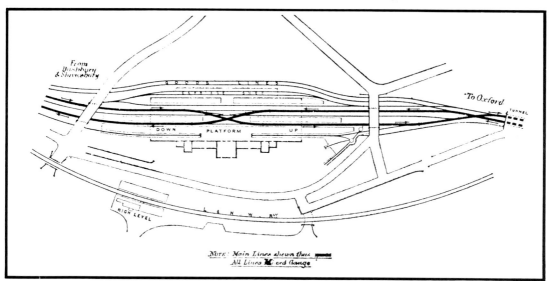

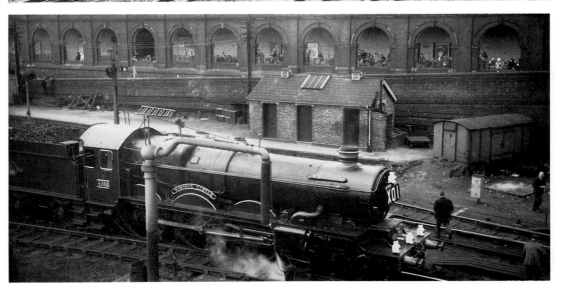

incomplete when the BW&D line opened on 14 November 1854, an event attended without ceremony, despite Brunel's presence. Temporary buildings were used on the site of the final station, leading to further confusion when these are referred to as a temporary station. The Low Level was probably completed towards the end of 1855, as in a report that February, Brunel noted that work on the station was 'in progress', but that it was 'yet incomplete'. A plan drawn in 1856, reproduced from McDermot, gives a good indication of the Joint station's layout when completed. That April, it was renamed the more familiar Wolverhampton Low Level.

The following description, from an 1860 directory, also gives a good idea of how the station appeared to its passengers:

'(It) presents in its very extended frontage a bold and graceful exemplification of Italian architecture; the blue bricks with which it is built throwing into cheerful relief the stone decorations of the edifice above, and sloping from which appears the imposing roof which covers the several platforms and lines of roadway beyond. The central portion of this building, from which the wings retreat, is devoted to the booking offices, which are so conveniently arranged as to leave entirely free for public accommodation a very large and lofty vestibule, on the sides of which, and separated so as to distribute the passengers, are the windows of the booking offices. Beyond the vestibule, and fronting a platform of unusual width, are the remainder of the offices, waiting and refreshment rooms. The extent of platform accommodation at this station is very considerable and contributes much to the merit of the general design – the great length of platforms enabling both up and down trains to arrive and start from one platform at the same time, and their great breadth preventing the possibility of crowding. Still more to increase the value of the space afforded, a light and graceful iron bridge, in the centre of the station, leads from the principal platform to a platform on the further side, which, during holiday periods, is made the departure side for excursion and special trains. Spanning these several platforms is an iron roof of great strength and elegant proportion.'

Over the next century the Low Level underwent considerable alterations. The first of these followed the official conversion of GWR Wolverhampton services to standard gauge on 1 April 1869. No longer required, the station's one-sidedness was removed. From opening, pedestrian communication with the LNWR's High Level station had been made through a dimly-lit tunnel known locally as 'The Brothel', due to its other night-time uses. With the

Below:
Plan of Wolverhampton Low Level in 1962.

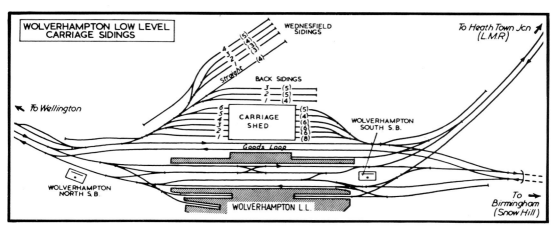

expansion of the High Level in 1884, this tunnel was extended some 36ft and provided with better lighting; the steps formerly at the Low Level end being replaced by a gradual arcaded incline known as 'The Colonnades'. Major trackwork alterations were made to the lines through Low Level during the fortnight 9/23 April 1899 in connection with the opening of a new carriage shed and sidings to the rear of the Birmingham or up platform. This work included the realignment of the station's goods avoiding lines and the commissioning of new North and South signalboxes to replace the existing North, Middle and South boxes.

Minor alterations were made over the next 20 years or so, including the strengthening of the passenger footbridge in 1902 to withstand the increased traffic from the town's Art & Industrial Exhibition, and an extension to the south end of the up platform in January 1911. But the main fabric of the station buildings remained more or less as built, until, that is, a major refurbishment scheme was begun towards the end of 1922. Under this, a new

booking office was created within the booking hall, having five ticket windows; a new telegraph department was added adjoining this in the former stationmaster's office, the waiting and refreshment rooms on both platforms were extended, and the passenger footbridge was replaced.

Attention was also paid to the 575ft long, 115ft span, 400-ton overall roof. Steam and heat create

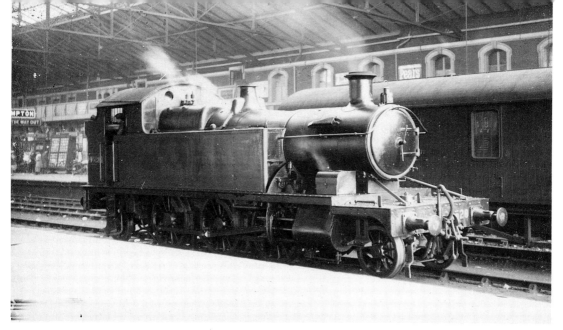

Above:
GWR 2-6-2T No 4528, one of the first lot of the '45XX'
class not to be built at Wolverhampton, waits at Low
Level around 1925. This shows the light and airy
qualities of the station's overall roof, which was
removed in 1934. *R. S. Carpenter*

ideal conditions to corrode iron, and 23 of the roof
purlins had succumbed to their effects, requiring
replacement. Sadly, this work did little to arrest the
roof's decay. In London or Bristol this roof would
have been acclaimed, but in Wolverhampton? More
repairs sustained it for a few years, but these were
too little, and too late. By 1933 its condition had
deteriorated so much that the GWR Divisional
Engineer decided that it would have to be removed.
After being photographed for posterity on 2 October,
the local contractors Wilson Lovatt & Co began to
dismantle the roof. So as not to interfere with the
working of the station, the method of demolition
employed was to build a temporary wooden
covering, running on rails fixed to the platforms,
which was advanced as the old roof was dismantled;
the replacement standard GWR platform canopies
being erected in the space this left behind. About
25ft of the old roof was dismantled each week, and
the work, which included a complete repaint for the
station, was completed by early May 1934.

Other alterations made to the Low Level were
relatively minor and included the replacement of gas
lighting with electricity in March 1930, the installation of an automatic telephone switchboard in
August 1932, alterations to the Telegraph Office in
October 1941, installation of two-ton electric goods
lifts in July 1944, and extensions for additional
engineer's accommodation in December 1952.

Wolverhampton Low Level saw its fair share of
excitement over the years, including no fewer than
three visits from Queen Victoria; the most notable
being that made on 30 November 1866, when Her
Majesty travelled from Windsor by the broad gauge,
behind 4-2-2 locomotive *Lord of the Isles,* driven by
Joseph Armstrong, late of Stafford Road locomotive
works. In later years, an unexpected visit from a
'king' (of the jungle) enlivened a Sunday afternoon,
when, on 9 December 1934, a lion, being unloaded
there for an appearance at Carmo's Circus, broke out
of its cage and stampeded about the train. Quickly
tamed by Mr Carmo himself, the Circus owner
proffered the explanation that the animal, a young
Abyssinian lion, was unused to rail travel; which is
almost as irresistible as the headline over this story,
as reported in the *GWR Magazine*: 'Thrills at
Wolverhampton'.

Stafford Road and Oxley Sheds

Wolverhampton's first 'GWR' engine sheds were
modest. The S&B opened a shed as part of its repair
works on Stafford Road around November 1849;
whilst in 1854 the OWW opened a small three-road
shed on land southeast of the Low Level station, by
the mouth of the tunnel that brought its line in from
Priestfield, around the same time the GWR proper
opened a three-road shed on the opposite side of
Stafford Road to accommodate broad gauge locomotives using its BW&D line. Situated in an area
later to be known as the Lower Yard, there were on
2 November 1860, 14 broad gauge locomotives
noted: three passenger tanks, two goods locomotives, six Birmingham passenger locomotives,
two Leamington passenger tanks, and one Stratford
coupled passenger tank.

Close to this, in 1860, the GWR built the first of three turntable sheds, to accommodate standard gauge locomotives. This could accommodate about 28 locomotives and in later years it became known as No 1 Shed. Between this and the broad gauge shed, which was converted to mixed gauge at around this time, ran two tracks, leading, as the repair works began to spill over into the lower yard, to the coppersmith's shop. During the mid-1860s, these tracks were roofed over to provide further covered accommodation for standard gauge locomotives, under what became known as 'The Arcade', or in later days No 4 Shed.

Following amalgamation with the WM in 1863, the original OWW shed was retained for a few years due to its proximity to the Low Level station, but was closed about 1872, its allocation being transferred to the Stafford Road Lower Yard sheds. By this time these were becoming somewhat overcrowded, especially following the conversion in 1869 of the original broad gauge shed into a tender shop, for the expanding locomotive works. Covered locomotive accommodation was urgently needed, and so two further turntable sheds were planned, to be built alongside shed No 1 of 1860. These became sheds Nos 2 and 3, and were built in 1874 and 1875, accommodating about 22 and 30 locomotives respectively. A 275ft-long straight shed was also built at the rear of, and with access from, the latter, in the early 1880s. This replaced a running shed built near to the end of Oxley Viaduct in 1858, which was then demolished. This brought the total capacity of the Stafford Road sheds up to almost 100 locomotives.

Left:
The street entrance to Stafford Road shed. The single-storey building to the right is the end of No 1 shed, built about 1860. *British Rail/OPC EO/487*

Below:
Stafford Road shed around 1883. The original broad gauge shed is at the extreme left; and the line of tenders is awaiting attention in the tender shop of the adjoining Locomotive works, which was by then sited in this Lower Yard area.
L&GRP, courtesy David & Charles (15741)

Above:
The two roads running in between No 1 shed and the former broad gauge shed at Stafford Road were roofed over in the mid-1860s to provide additional covered accommodation. This became known as 'The Arcade' or No 4 shed, where No 7026 *Sudeley Castle* and No 6969 *Wraysbury Hall* seek shelter in the late 1950s.
F. Braybrook

Right:
The inside of one of Oxley's two turntable sheds, pictured when new around 1908.
Wolverhampton Library

No further development took place on the Stafford Road shed site for about 25 years until the installation of a larger turntable in 1900, which enabled 4-2-2s to work to Wolverhampton; 'Achilles' class Nos 3015 and 3050 being regularly seen there. The shed also accommodated some of the GWR's new Steam Rail Motor cars, which were introduced into the area in 1905 to work local services between Wolverhampton and Albrighton. By this time, Stafford Road shed was at capacity, all the other suitable land in the Lower Yard site having been taken up by the locomotive works. Yet Wolverhampton was fast becoming one of the busiest operating depots in the country!

A solution to the problem of congestion was found late in 1905, when readers of the *GWR Magazine* were informed that 'The Directors have recently authorised the erection of engine sheds at Oxley and Small Heath. These sheds represent standard Great Western practice, as laid down by Mr Churchward, and will be similar to the one recently erected at Old Oak Common, which is on the internal turntable principle with radial pits.' This site lay on the down side of the line at Oxley sidings, about a mile from the GWR's Dunstall Park station. The contract for its erection was let in March 1906 to the Wolverhampton firm of Henry Lovatt, which is mentioned in more detail in Chapter 6. On this narrow site, two 65ft turntables were placed one behind the other; each encircled by 28 pits, varying from 41ft to 100ft in length. These afforded accommodation for about 30

Above:
The coaling stage at Oxley shed on 20 June 1964, with an unidentified 57XX 0-6-0PT and No 7828 *Odney Manor*. Only the one side of this coaler was ever fitted out, although it was built to have an identical stage on the opposite side. *Simon Dewey*

tender and 30 tank locomotives each. Both units of the shed were fed by their own in and outgoing roads, the front of the leading shed also having a repair shop and offices projecting from it. A coal stage was situated in front of the sheds, with two water tanks on top, having a total capacity of 145,000gal. Both this, and the sheds, were designed with the intention of adding two further sheds at a later date, if the extra capacity was required. It was not, and the perfectly symmetrical coal stage was only ever fitted out on one side.

Oxley shed opened on 1 July 1907, and was operated jointly with Stafford Road shed; the latter tending to concentrate upon servicing the larger passenger express locomotives that required a quick turn-around before a return trip to Paddington, given its proximity to the Low Level station. As such, it was probably Stafford Road shed that accommodated the following modern passenger locomotives in the autumn of 1913: Atlantic 4-4-2 No 104 *Alliance*, 4-6-0s Nos 2901 *Lady Superior*, 2902 *Lady of the Lake*, 2905 *Lady Macbeth*, 2906 *Lady of Lynn*, 2908 *Lady of Quality*, 2909 *Lady of Provence*, 2910 *Lady of Shalott*, 2911 *Saint Agatha* and 2949 *Stanford Court*; four-cylinder classes Nos 4004 *Morning Star*, 4034 *Adelaide* and 4036 *Elizabeth*.

Oxley's opening led to some spare capacity at Stafford Road shed, which, apart from minor alterations, such as the extension of the four engine pits in No 5 shed to accommodate an extra locomotive each, in November 1923, fell into disrepair. Following a reorganisation of the adjacent repair works, completed in 1932, the former broad gauge shed was brought back into use as a running shed, the Road Motor Department taking over shed No 3; shed No 2 continuing in use until the late

1940s, despite having all but lost its roof. These trends were reflected in the shed's allocations, when in 1946, Stafford Road had 74 locomotives and Oxley 99.

Material decline having set in, it continued after nationalisation, with the reroofing of the 'broad gauge' shed and the adjoining 'Arcade', with corrugated iron sheeting in the 1950s. This was the only attention Stafford Road shed received before closure. April 1948 also saw BR adopt a new Motive Power Depot numbering system, based on that formerly used by the LMS. Under this system, Stafford Road shed (SRD under the GWR coding system), became No 84A, and Oxley (OXY) No 84B.

Appendix 3 contains a digest of the GWR's official statistics, showing the operation of its Wolverhampton Division sheds over equivalent weeks in June 1936 and June 1937.

The Bridgnorth & Wolverhampton Railway

The stagecoach and horse omnibus services from Wolverhampton to Bridgnorth were the last to operate in the town, the length and rural nature of the route not lending itself to any other form of transport. The GWR had stations in both towns, but travelling between them by rail was far from direct, being either via Shrewsbury or Kidderminster. Recognising that revenue was being lost through

Above:
GWR 4-6-0 No 2902 *Lady of the Lake* was one of no fewer than eight sister engines allocated to Wolverhampton in the autumn of 1913. *LPC*

Bottom:
GWR No 2257, with an ex-ROD tender, shunts coal wagons at Stafford Road shed's coaling stage in the 1930s. *F. Braybrook*

this, the GWR introduced a bus service between the two towns from 7 November 1904 using three paraffin-fired single-deck Clarkson steam buses. Local hills defeated these, and they were replaced by petrol-driven buses from 10 April 1905. A service of four of these, each way, proved so successful over

the 14-mile/90min journey that two additional buses were run each way over branch routes opened to Pattingham, in May 1906, and to Claverley, in December 1911.

These services had been inaugurated in lieu of building a railway between Bridgnorth and Wolverhampton, a line of that name (B&W) having been authorised on 11 July 1905, under that year's GWR (New Railways) Act. As shown, this was to unite two lines near Trysull, a new one, running south from Wolverhampton (Dunstall Park) and a continuation of the ex-OWW Kingswinford branch (opened on 14 November 1858), with a new line to join the GWR's Severn Valley line at Bridgnorth. This route was altered under the GWR Act of 18 June 1908, diverting the line through Wombourn. Construction

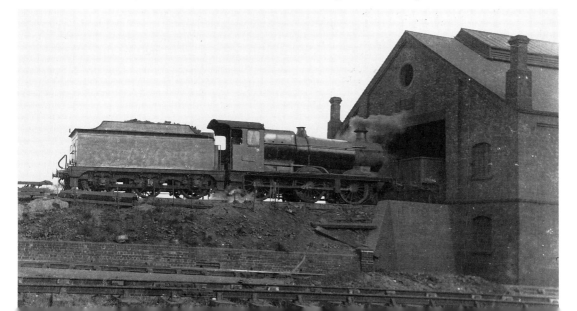

Above:
Stafford Road shed's well tended turntable is pressed into use turning ex-GWR No 5015 *Kingswear Castle* on 20 July 1954. Notice the shed's coaling stage at the extreme right, and the jaunty angle of the telegraph pole behind! *Brian Morrison*

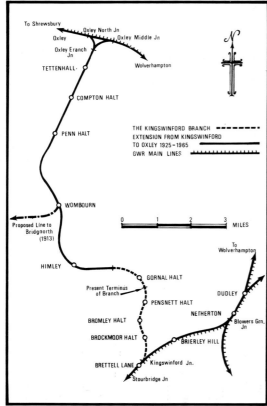

Above:
The Wombourn line.

was delayed through negotiations with the Earl of Dudley, who was planning to expand his colliery operations on the adjacent Pensnett Chase coalfield. In order to combine serving these with building the new line, it was decided to concentrate initial construction work upon its Kingswinford-Wolverhampton section.

The GWR Act passed in June 1913 further revised the B&W scheme; work on the line to Bridgnorth being officially postponed. Contractors began work that autumn, continuing until sometime in 1916, when wartime shortages of men and materials became acute. They resumed work, in a somewhat piecemeal fashion, after the war, but abandoned it in the spring of 1920, auctioning their plant over 12-13 May that year. The GWR assumed the task of completing the line in the middle of 1921, although its Board only authorised the additional £173,000 expenditure this required under an Act passed on 29 June 1923.

Much of the work was at its northern end, the junction with the ex-S&B line at Oxley being opened on 11 January 1925, along with a new signalbox to control this, Oxley North Box, the former North box becoming 'Oxley Middle Box'. Finally completed, passenger services between Stourbridge Junction and Wolverhampton Low Level via Wombourn

Above:
Stafford Road shed's yard in the early 1960s, with No 6148, 'Castle' Class No 5052 *Earl of Radnor*, **and No 6002** *King William IV.* *Wolverhampton Chronicle*

Right:
The GWR handed its Bridgnorth bus service to Wolverhampton Corporation from 1 July 1923. Corporation bus No 185 is seen waiting to depart for Bridgnorth from in front of Low Level on Christmas Eve 1929. *Bennett Clark/Author's Collection*

Below right:
GWR Steam Rail Motor No 40 was photographed at Tettenhall station on the opening day of the 'Wombourn' line, 11 May 1925, by an amateur cameraman. One can tell it's not an official photograph — the staff are smiling!
P. Eisenhoffer/Wolverhampton Library

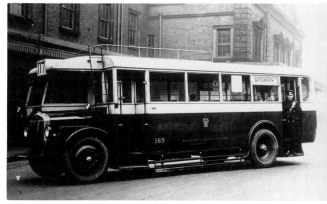

began on 11 May 1925 and were operated by Steam Rail Motor cars. From the continuation of the Kingswinford branch there were stations at Himley, Wombourn, Penn Halt, Compton Halt and Tettenhall; the cars operating into a bay at the Shrewsbury end of the down platform at Low Level station.

Passenger loadings on these services were always lower than expected. Through passengers from Wolverhampton to Stourbridge could use the established ex-OWW route, which was both 9min quicker and served more populous towns en route; and the majority of those served by the B&W's halts and stations had little need to travel anywhere that it went. In fact, the line had been completed more for the sake of doing so than to meet any real need, other than for goods services; a branch to serve the large

Courtaulds factory at Dunstall Hall opening in August 1927. With little surprise therefore, passenger services were withdrawn on 31 October 1932.

From then, the B&W line saw only occasional passenger services, other than non-stopping diversions. Between 6 and 10 July 1937, Tettenhall station reopened to serve passengers for the Royal Agricultural Society's Show, held that year in Wrottesley Park Wolverhampton; an additional platform and siding being added for the occasion. During World War 2, D-Day wounded were brought by 40 or so trains to New Cross Hospital in Wolverhampton, being offloaded at Tettenhall and Wombourn stations. But the real measure of demand for the line is seen in the response to a public meeting held in Wombourn on 30 June 1961 to discuss the prospects of reopening it to passengers; 25 attended!

Oxley and Cannock Road Sidings

Having come second to Wolverhampton, and having arrived secondhand as it were, it took the GWR a

while to get certain aspects of its operations there in full order. One such aspect was the provision of sidings for the storage of wagon and carriage stock.

Until the 1870s, the storage and shunting of goods wagons was shared with the LNWR at their Bushbury exchange sidings, just north of the Stour Valley/GJR junction there, and alongside Bushbury shed. The GWR gained the right to use these sidings through its amalgamation with the West Midland

Below:
Wombourn station on 17 August 1957 as ex-GWR No 6910 *Fron Hall* brings the stock from the 9.35am Bournemouth Central-Wolverhampton Low Level on an ecs return working to Henley-on-Thames.
G. F. Bannister

Bottom:
An Oxley sidings-Baggeridge Junction local goods waits for BR Standard Class 4 4-6-0 No 75024 to clear the single line with an empty ballast train on 24 April 1957.
G. F. Bannister

RAILWAY ARCHES.

Railway in 1863; the original agreement with the LNWR being made by the OWW at a site meeting at

Above:
Oxley Viaduct photographed at the start of the century showing the skewed arch built to allow the Birmingham Canal to pass underneath. It is worth spending a few moments considering the skill required to build this. The signals are also impressive. *Eric Hamilton Collection*

Below:
Although this print of the north end of Oxley sidings c1897 has deteriorated over the years, it is included to show the remodelling and expansion work undertaken there that year. The old North signalbox can be seen through the murk on the right, and the base of its replacement is taking shape at the extreme right. Note the dumb-buffered wagons in the siding.
Wolverhampton Library

Bushbury Junction on 24 March 1854. At this meeting, the LNWR agreed to more than double its siding accommodation at Bushbury to allow for the reception of OWW traffic, the work being completed by the end of April 1854. Then, Bushbury exchange sidings comprised seven lines, four being off the 'To Stafford' line and three off the 'From Stafford' line.

It is not known whether the GWR made use of these sidings prior to 1863, although, with the management of Low Level station resting in a Joint Committee on which its representatives sat, this is perfectly possible. But from 1863 onwards the GWR made extensive use of the sidings. Shunting wagons in the four line sidings was the GWR's responsibility as follows: No 1 for Manchester; Manchester Sheffield & Lincolnshire Railway (MSLR), and Lancashire & Yorkshire Railway (LYR); No 2 for Liverpool, Crewe and destinations to Scotland; No 3

for Birkenhead, plus North Staffordshire Railway (NSR) and Shropshire Union Company; No 4 empties for Ulverstone, plus empties for the Shrewsbury & Hereford line, LNWR, and all private owner empties. Correspondingly, the LNWR shunted all wagons in the three line sidings thus: No 1 for Worcester and beyond, plus Midland railway empties; No 2 for all stations between Bushbury and Droitwich, and No 3 for all West Midland Section empties and mineral wagons.

Sometime during the 1870s new goods sidings were laid out at Oxley on the ex-S&B line, commencing a few yards or so from the end of the viaduct which carries the line over the Birmingham Canal. Initially there were just four sidings on either side of the running lines, set out in a near symmetrical arrangement, controlled by Oxley North and Oxley South signalboxes. Soon proven to be inadequate, these were considerably expanded under work completed in October 1897 which also involved the relocation of both signalboxes. Further alterations followed the building of Oxley shed on vacant land in the down yard during 1906-07.

In their final form Oxley sidings had 23 lines on the up side, divided into three sections: the Old Yard which consisted of 10 sidings holding 608 wagons for local traffic; the Middle Sidings, of two lines holding 32 wagons for down traffic; and the New Yard, 11 sidings holding 656 wagons for the marshalling of main line through traffic. The down side had 17 lines, in two sections: the Crewe Yard of eight lines holding 315 wagons for local up traffic and that for Crewe, and the Birkenhead Yard which consisted of nine sidings holding 333 wagons for the Shrewsbury and Birkenhead lines, giving an overall capacity of 1,944 wagons.

Limited carriage accommodation had been provided at the Low Level station, to the rear of the up lines and excursion platforms. This was replaced and greatly expanded by April 1899 under work already described and further supplemented by three new carriage sidings, built off the Cannock Road Junction-Bushbury Junction connecting line in 1900. Being situated in between the Low Level station and Stafford Road shed, these sidings allowed carriages to be stored conveniently for locomotives going on or coming off the shed, to drop or collect them. Six additional sidings were added, alongside the above-mentioned connecting line, about March 1936, for the stabling of longer sets of coaches; the sidings by the Low Level station being restricted to sets of six coaches or shorter, most for local workings.

A diesel fuelling point was installed at Cannock Road Carriage sidings to service the DMUs introduced in the Wolverhampton area of the WR in 1957. These used sidings 1 and 2 in the 'New' group; No 3 being used by the Birmingham Pullman diesel set. Cannock Road sidings could accommodate 46 65ft-carriages in the old sidings, and 84 in the new, the shunting neck accommodating nine coaches, plus a locomotive, clear of the carriage siding points. All of these sidings were equipped with gassing, battery charging and watering facilities. In 1958, the Cannock Road Junction-Bushbury Junction connecting line ceased to be used as a freight exchange point between BR(WR) and BR(LMR); its running lines then becoming available for the storage of up

to 40 carriages each. With the Old Goods sidings also taking 17 coaches, this brought the total capacity of Cannock Road Carriage sidings up to 227; the Low Level sidings holding an extra 68.

The Development of Passenger Services

Wolverhampton is often quoted as being the headquarters of the GWR's Northern Division, which it was, in locomotive matters. Operationally, under the Traffic Department, the town did indeed initially come under the Northern Division when this was formed in 1854, following the absorption of the Shrewsbury railways. Then the headquarters was at Shrewsbury, until it was moved to Chester in December 1860. The GWR's Traffic Department was reorganised in 1865-66, Wolverhampton thereafter coming under a newly formed Birmingham Division, which also assumed the responsibilities of an abolished Dudley Division.

1 — The development of local passenger services

In the early days of rail travel, excursions were used to attract passengers to the railways who might otherwise have had no reason to travel. One such excursion ran from Wolverhampton to Worcester on 23 August 1858, a Bank Holiday Monday. The outward train was so long that it returned as two trains (1st 28 carriages, two brake vans; 2nd 14 carriages, two brake vans). Taking on an additional locomotive at Stourbridge, the first train proceeded to Round Oak station where it stopped to set passengers down. Unfortunately, the guard applied the brake so violently that a coupling snapped, and the rear 17 carriages were sent back down the 1 in 75 gradient into the path of the second train. They collided at Moor Lane Bridge, just north of Brettell Lane station, the rear van and end three carriages being smashed to splinters. Eleven died instantly, three more later from their injuries, a further 170 being injured. An inauspicious start, but something, mercifully, not to be repeated.

The more regular service over the OWW/WM line is indicated by the latter's timetable for August 1862 which shows 11 departures from Wolverhampton Low Level: four to Oxford (fastest 3hr 25min, slowest 4hr 35min); one to Evesham (2hr 20min); one to Worcester (1hr 40min); two to Hartlebury (1hr 30min); one to Kidderminster (1hr 5min) and two to Dudley (25min).

On the ex-S&B line, a stopping service was provided by trains working through to Liverpool or Manchester, with Albrighton having additional stopping trains on market days; there being 19 such trains daily, 10 up, 9 down in 1865. The busiest local line was the BW&D into Birmingham. Some measure of the passenger business this generated can be taken from the GWR's introduction of season or 'Periodical' tickets from the Low Level to local stations to Birmingham from 1 October 1859. By 1865, there were 27 daily local trains along this line, 14 up, 13 down, each taking between 45min and 50min for the journey. These were all broad gauge trains, some having worked through from Leamington Spa, Stratford-on-Avon, Knowle or Solihull.

All Wolverhampton-Birmingham local trains began running on the narrow gauge from 1 November 1868, although the pattern of services remained very similar, despite the more generous timings the GWR typically allowed its narrow gauge trains. The same holds true for the pattern of the GWR's other local services, particularly the ex-WM ones; this being operated as a more or less self-contained 'West Midland Section' for a number of years.

Eight years after the opening of Wolverhampton's new racecourse the GWR opened a station to serve it on 1 December 1896. This was situated on the Stafford Road, near the Stafford Road Junction end of the Cannock Road Junction S&B link line, opened in November 1854. In addition to local passengers, and serving employees of the GWR's locomotive works, Dunstall Park station served to relieve the Low Level of race day excursions and additional passengers carried annually to the town's Flower Show and its Fete, both held there. This station also represented quite a steal on the LNWR, whose High Level station was over a mile from the racecourse.

From 1900, to the end of the period under consideration, the basic core of services described was maintained, with slight variations. Up to World War 2 the GWR's Wolverhampton-Birmingham passenger traffic grew steadily; thus in 1902 there were 43 trains daily (22 up, 21 down), and by 1932 there were 49 (25 up, 24 down), many of these being extended through workings of North Warwickshire line trains. The majority of these called at all local stations as the following figures for 1914 show: Priestfield (15 up, 15 down), Bilston (21 up, 22 down), Bradley & Moxley (13 up, 11 down), Wednesbury (22 up, 24 down).

Services calling at local stations to Shrewsbury also increased slightly, with additional short workings to Albrighton and Shifnal being added from the introduction of Steam Rail Motors in 1905. But the greatest increase in service frequency was seen on the ex-OWW line, whose local stations came to be served by an average of 39 trains (20 up, 19 down), including one each way that worked through to Paddington.

Before the 1960s, only one 19th century GWR Wolverhampton local station closed completely, this was Bradley & Moxley, on 1 May 1915, initially as a wartime economy measure, although both the GWR and local people soon found that they could live

Below:
Dunstall Park station was opened by the GWR on 1 December 1896 and is seen here on 30 March 1957 with ex-GWR 4-4-0 No 3440 *City of Truro* passing through on a Festiniog Railway Special. Notice the platform signalbox and the elegant cast iron gents.
G. F. Bannister

The booking office at Dunstall Park station was situated at road level. This view of ex-GWR No 6861 *Crynant Grange*, passing through the station in the early 1960s, shows the buildings that were situated at track level. *J. B. Bucknall*

without it. For similar reasons Dunstall Park was also closed on 1 January 1917 but was reopened on 3 March 1919. In addition, all of the stations on the B&W Wombourn line came and went within this period, its final timetable having only 14 trains (seven up, seven down), three of which were short workings to and from Wombourn, two of these being in the middle of the day; the service being operated by Steam Rail Motors from Stourbridge Junction.

During the 1930s, in order to compete with increasing competition from motor buses, the GWR invested heavily in the building of new quickly-erected stations. Usually unstaffed and situated adjacent to new housing developments, these stations were given the status of halts; the idea being that if they generated a good deal of new traffic their somewhat basic facilities could be improved, and if they failed to do so they could be closed and removed at little cost. The first such station in the Wolverhampton area was Birches & Bilbrook Halt, sited between Dunstall Park and Codsall stations on the S&B line, which had staggered platforms and opened on 30 April 1934; it was served by the majority of the local trains between Wolverhampton and Wellington.

Four years later Cosford Aerodrome Halt, situated between Albrighton and Shifnal stations on the S&B line, was opened on 31 January 1938 to serve the

personnel of an aerodrome then under construction there in the Air Ministry's build-up to the coming war. Cosford's traffic increased rapidly and in August 1939 the *Railway Gazette* announced that facilities at the halt were to be improved by the construction of booking, waiting, parcels, lavatory and cycle storage areas. With these completed, Cosford was converted to a full station, and renamed thus on 28 October 1940. Both Cosford station and Birches & Bilbrook Halt proved themselves viable and have remained open, unlike New Hadley Halt, between Oakengates and Wellington, which was opened on 3 November 1934 but was closed by British Rail from 13 May 1985.

World War 2 brought slight service reductions on all of the GWR's local Wolverhampton lines, which had not returned to their prewar service levels by the time of nationalisation. This heralded a period of station refurbishment, which began with the repainting of Bilston station, on the ex-OWW line (later Bilston West), on 6 January 1948.

Excepting the July 1950 station name changes already mentioned, there were few changes to the pre-nationalisation service pattern prior to the introduction of DMUs on local Western Region services from 17 June 1957; from when these units, with their quick turn-around ability, allowed some increases in passenger services between Wolverhampton and Wellington, and along the ex-BW&D line to Birmingham, although 10 lightly loaded Birmingham Western Region local services, including some to Wolverhampton, were cut-out in the first major reorganisation these had received since nationalisation; which took effect from 5 March 1962.

Sadly, the DMUs came too late to prevent the withdrawal of passenger services between Wolverhampton and Stourbridge Junction. The line had enjoyed little support from local people, particularly in Stourbridge, who felt the Low Level station to be inconvenient for Wolverhampton and were also well served by local buses and by trolleybuses from Dudley. With the increase in private car ownership during the 1950s, the Stourbridge-Wolverhampton line's days were numbered and services were withdrawn from 30 July 1962, all of the stations between Stourbridge Junction and Priestfield, with the exception of Dudley, closing to passengers from that day.

Above:
With a little over six weeks left to run, Oswestry shed's 'Castle' Class No 5070 *Sir Daniel Gooch* waits to depart a quiet Wolverhampton Low Level with the 2.10pm local service to Stourbridge Junction via the ex-OWW main line on 11 June 1962. Passenger services over the line ceased from 30 July 1962. *Michael Mensing*

Below:
Another Wolverhampton local turn that ended in July 1962 was the Saturdays-only through working of the 12.03pm Low Level to Old Hill service, which ran via the ex-OWW line to Dudley. The last working of this service was captured at Old Hill on 14 July 1962. What happened to the pigeons after this? *Leslie Sandler*

2 — Express passenger services

Wolverhampton's first long-distance 'GWR' services (given their journey times they can hardly be called expresses) began on 1 April 1854. As *The Times* reported that 30 March, the OWW company

'has just entered into a traffic agreement with the LNWR, which will come into operation on Saturday next, and by which trains will run direct daily to and from London (Euston-square) and Wolverhampton by way of the Buckinghamshire line, Oxford, Chipping Campden, Worcester, Kidderminster and Dudley, etc. Five trains will run daily throughout, and eight trains will run daily between Worcester and Wolverhampton. Four trains, via the Great Western Railway, run daily between Paddington and Wolverhampton along the Oxford, Worcester and Wolverhampton line.'

This had been made possible by the opening of two lengths of line connecting the OWW and LNWR: the Tipton Curve (opened 1 December 1853), and a 1¾-mile branch from the LNWR's Bletchley-Bicester-Oxford line to the OWW at Yarnton (opened 1 April 1854); the former having allowed Wolverhampton-Worcester-Oxford services to commence.

The Times' report was accompanied by a time-table which seems to be a little at variance with it. Nonetheless, any confusion here does not diminish the intrigue that surrounds the last sentence in the report; which, in its use of the present tense 'run', implies that GWR trains were already running the whole journey between Paddington and Wolverhampton. Of course, this is nonsense. The GWR was broad gauge to Oxford, and even at this time was pursuing a Bill through Parliament to force the OWW to complete laying the broad gauge along its line. What we have here is Victorian journalist's license. The GWR had commenced an Oxford-Paddington service on 1 December 1853, to connect with the OWW's Wolverhampton trains, and it is this that is being referred to; a view supported by the wording of an OWW advertisement which states that passengers will be carried 'without break of gauge or change of carriage'.

The joint OWW/LNWR trains ran until 30 September 1861, through running of narrow gauge Worcester-Paddington trains commencing the following day, the LNWR also re-routeing its statutory third-class 'Parliamentary' trains, which it had run to Wolverhampton via the OWW line to reduce congestion on its main L&B line. Three years later, on 1 January 1864, the GWR began running a service of two through trains each way, to and from Manchester London Road, via the LNWR, which was joined via the Cannock Road Junction-Bushbury

OXFORD, WORCESTER, and WOLVER-HAMPTON RAILWAY.—On and after Saturday, the 1st of April, 1854, passengers will be booked and conveyed throughout, without break of gauge or change of carriage, between Euston Station, London, and stations on the Oxford, Worcester and Wolverhampton Railway, by the following trains:—

WEEK DAYS.
Down Trains.

—	Express. 1st and 2d class.	Ordinary. 1st and 2d class.	Express. 1st and 2 1 class.
Leave London	9.30 a.m.	1.45 p.m.	5.15 p.m.
Arrive at Worcester	1. 0 p.m.	6.45 p.m.	8.50 p.m.
„ Kidderminster ..	1.38 p.m.	7.25 p.m.	9.30 p.m.
„ Stourbridge ..	1.50 p.m.	7.40 p.m.	9.43 p.m.
„ Dudley	2. 5 p.m.	8. 0 p.m.	10. 0 p.m.

WEEK DAYS.
Up Trains.

—	Express. 1st and 2d class.	Ordinary. 1st and 2d class.	Express. 1st and 2d class.
Leave Dudley	6 30 a.m.	10.25 a.m.	4.40 p.m.
„ Stourbridge	6.45 a.m.	10.45 a.m.	4.55 p.m.
„ Kidderminster	6.58 a.m.	11. 5 a.m.	5. 8 p.m.
„ Worcester	7.30 a.m.	12. 0 noon.	5.40 p.m.
Arrive at London	11.15 a.m.	5. 0 p.m.	9.15 p.m.

By order, W. T. ADCOCK.

Above:

The OWW timetable for the joint LNWR Wolverhampton High Level-Euston service which began on 1 April 1854. *Author's Collection*

line; the only regular passenger traffic this line ever saw, the service ceasing on 30 September 1867.

Wolverhampton's first real GWR expresses were those over the BW&D, B&O, and O&R lines to Paddington via Didcot. Paddington to Birmingham expresses had been running since 1 October 1852 and had the potential to work through to Wolverhampton with the opening of the BW&D line on 14 November 1854, although references in GWR minutes suggest that, at least initially, a Wolverhampton connection may have been provided by local broad gauge services or by Shrewsbury line trains working through to Birmingham on the narrow gauge. Such arrangements may have been necessary pending the establishment of adequate broad gauge locomotive and carriage facilities at Wolverhampton. On the broad gauge, the Paddington to Birmingham expresses were initially scheduled to do the trip in 2hr 45min, but this was a little ambitious and they were rescheduled to 3hr dead, to match the corresponding LNWR Euston-Birmingham expresses; the leg to Wolverhampton being covered in about 25min nonstop.

The story of the development of this express service is really another one of rivalry with the LNWR. In spite of a disadvantage to be mentioned later, the GWR was quite capable of matching the LNWR almost minute for minute on any improvements it may have introduced. Consequently, readers can check that almost all reduced timings, improved standards of service, etc, were introduced on the same date, by both companies. Occasionally though, one took a small lead, such as when the GWR reduced its time to Birmingham to 2hr 50min from 1 March 1859, and the LNWR's remained at 3hr.

As the GWR opened more narrow gauge routes, such as that to South Wales via Worcester and Hereford, on 18 April 1864, the broad gauge service to Wolverhampton became increasingly isolated. This restricted the planning of through services, and was resented by passengers who had to change trains to continue their journeys. More and more broad gauge duties were changed over to narrow gauge working, until, from 1 November 1868, only the 7.00pm Wolverhampton-Paddington and the 6.15pm Paddington-Wolverhampton services remained over the broad gauge. These finally ceased officially from 1 April 1869 although individual trains and occasional stock movements may have continued to use the broad gauge lines for some time after this date.

The 1870s was a difficult decade for the GWR, and its attention was diverted away from the West Midlands. A massive programme of gauge conversion was undertaken in the West and in South Wales, but north of Oxford no improvements were made. Only one train a day offered travel to Birmingham in under 3hr, the others taking between 3hr 20min and 4hr. There were many problems, not the least of which was the state of the track. Much of this was the older style 'baulk road', the broad gauge type of bridge rail laid on longitudinal sleepers, which many drivers said was 'stiff' and harder to work, and they reckoned it to be like hauling an extra two carriages compared to a train on transverse-sleepered track.

The first signs of improvement came on 1 June 1880, with the introduction of the 4.45pm Paddington-Birkenhead express which reached Wolverhampton in 3hr 4min and Birkenhead in 5hr 17min. This became known as the 'Zulu', or sometimes the 'Afghan' or 'Northern Zulu', to distinguish it from the Paddington-Penzance service which had been given this unofficial name when introduced one year earlier. The train was introduced at the height of the Zulu War, and Zulu warriors were reputed for their speed. The corre-

sponding up 'Zulu' started at Birkenhead at 11.45am, reaching Wolverhampton at 2.05pm and Paddington at 5.25pm; and both 'Zulus' always had a Wolverhampton locomotive in charge.

For most of the 1880s, the burden of working the Wolverhampton-Paddington expresses fell upon the GWR 7ft single locomotives from the '999' or '157' classes, the Wolverhampton pool of '999s': 1000, 1116, 1121, 1127; and 157: 160, 161 and 164, being the nine engines mainly responsible, typically being called upon to work the four daily turns to London. The others would also share duties over the West Midlands section, with its assortment of 12 or so ex-OWW and ex-NA&H small double-framed 2-4-0s. Most of the Didcot-Worcester-Wolverhampton services were worked by ex-WM rebuilt Beyer-Peacock engines Nos 196-201 and Nos 209-214; whilst trains north of Wolverhampton, to Chester and Birkenhead, were worked by a motley assortment of tank engines, mainly based at Chester, with 'Sir Daniel' class Nos 378, 473 and 578 being the only 7ft singles to run north of Wolverhampton.

It took nearly a decade for Wolverhampton's expresses to improve. In 1889 an extra Paddington express was introduced to supplement the six daily fasts that worked through to Shrewsbury, but it was not until July 1891 that three additional expresses were introduced to Paddington, in response to LNWR competition. From then improvements came more rapidly. The first GWR corridor train was introduced on 1 March 1892, on the 1.30pm Paddington-Birkenhead service, and in July 1896 a new service to North Wales via Wolverhampton commenced; 1 July 1898 seeing a new service to Liverpool Central (Low Level) via the Mersey Tunnel begin. Journey times started to tumble. A nonstop Paddington-Birmingham express was inaugurated

Below:
GWR '999' class No 999 *Sir Alexander*, **one of the nine 7ft singles on to which the burden of working most of the Wolverhampton-Paddington expresses fell in the 1880s, is seen on Stafford Road shed. No 999 achieved a mileage of 1,329,000, the highest of its class, before withdrawal in October 1904.** *LPC*

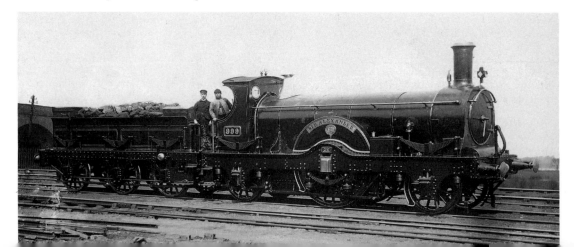

on 1 July 1898, completing the run in 2hr 27min, 2min being taken off this in 1899 and 4min more in 1901.

Water troughs had been installed to remove stops en route to Birmingham, but other improvements brought new problems. The GWR's new 70ft 'Dreadnought' coaches, introduced on 1 July 1904, were, at 9ft 6in, too wide to work north of Wolverhampton, limiting them to the Paddington expresses. With faster working now possible, the GWR became interested in attracting Liverpool 'American' boat passengers, and ran a number of special timing runs between Paddington and Birkenhead in 1905. These ran nonstop, save for a change of locomotive at Wolverhampton. One such run, with passengers for SS *Calcutta* on 5 October 1905, ran from Paddington to Wolverhampton in 2hr 34min behind No 3405 *Mauritius*, and did Wolverhampton to Birkenhead in 1hr 41min behind No 3311 *Wynnstay*.

But no matter how many accelerations were made, the GWR was labouring under a severe handicap when competing with the LNWR to London. The latter's route from there to Wolverhampton was 125 miles and could be covered at best in 2hr 30min; whereas the GWR's piecemeal assemblage of a route to the town was 141¾ miles, which could not be covered in under 2hr 45min. Even greater problems existed between Wolverhampton, Birmingham and Bristol. Nothing approximating to a direct route existed, although 'West and North' expresses, between Bristol and Shrewsbury via the Severn Tunnel, had served Wolverhampton since 1 July 1888. A direct route from Bristol incorporating bits of existing lines was opened on 1 July 1908; a Wolverhampton-Bristol express service starting that day.

Ironing out the route from London was undertaken jointly with the Great Central Railway (GCR), which, although newly opened to London, needed an alternate approach to the capital to negate a growing dispute with the Metropolitan Railway over use of its joint line south from Quainton Road. Powers to build a new line, from the GCR at Grendon Underwood to the GWR at Princes Risborough, were obtained in 1899; this, together with an upgrading of the line from there to High Wycombe, satisfied the GCR. The GWR also planned a new line north from Princes Risborough, to a junction with their old line to Birmingham at Aynho — the Bicester cut-off, and built this under an Act of 11 July 1905; the line opening to passengers on 1 July 1910. The new route to Birmingham was 110½ miles long, 19 less than the old route via Oxford, and two miles less than the LNWR. It reduced the distance to Wolverhampton to 123 miles, and enabled expresses to run to Birmingham in 2hr.

The date 1 October 1910 was an important one for the development of GWR services from Wolverhampton as it saw the introduction of a number of joint services, all of which ran to or via there. Three were with the Midland: Weston-super-Mare–Birkenhead, Torquay-Wolverhampton and Penzance-Wolverhampton; with one up and one down train per day. Two joint services with the South Eastern & Chatham Railway (SECR) also began that day: the 'Continental Express', from Wolverhampton to London (Victoria) and on to Paris, in 11¾hr; plus a through service from Deal and Dover to Birkenhead.

Finally, jointly with the London & South Western Railway (LSWR) and the LNWR, a service was introduced between Bournemouth West and Manchester and Birkenhead. This was worked by the LSWR to Oxford, the GWR working it on to Wolverhampton where it was split; one portion going nonstop to Crewe via Wellington to be attached to an LNWR train to Manchester, the other being taken on by the GWR, stopping at major stations to Birkenhead. Returning, the two portions would be united at Wolverhampton. To supplement

Left:
GWR 'Bulldog' class No 3390 was named *Wolverhampton,* **but not after May 1927, when it, and all other similarly 'place-named' locomotives were condemned to obscurity on the pretext that passengers had become confused between the locomotives and their destinations! Where did they think sister engine No 3391** *Dominion of Canada* **was going to then?**
L&GRP, courtesy David & Charles (51224)

Below left:
Late 1950s express working at Wolverhampton Low Level is illustrated by this view of No 6861 *Crynant Grange* **on 12 September 1959 being detached from the 11.45 Birkenhead service in order that 'King' class No 6009** *King Charles II* **can be attached to take the train to Paddington.** *Michael Mensing*

Bottom left:
The official publicity photograph of the Birmingham 'Blue Pullman' set, taken on 2 May 1960, probably at High Wycombe. The Wolverhampton-Paddington Pullman service began on 12 September 1960. *BR*

Right:
The first timetable of the 'Birmingham Pullman' diesel service, which began on 12 September 1960.
Author's Collection

Bottom:
The 'Birmingham Pullman' stock seen at Wolverhampton Low Level in 1963. By this time 120 of its 220 seats were available to second-class passengers.
Eric Hamilton Collection

THE BIRMINGHAM PULLMAN
(LIMITED ACCOMMODATION)

LONDON, LEAMINGTON SPA, BIRMINGHAM and WOLVERHAMPTON

WEEK DAYS
(Mondays to Fridays)

		am	pm
Wolverhampton (Low Level)	dep	7 0	..
Birmingham (Snow Hill)	,,	7 30	2 30
Solihull	,,	7 40	..
Leamington Spa General	,,	8 0	2 55
London (Paddington)	arr	9 35	4 25

		pm	pm
London (Paddington)	dep	12 10	4 50
Leamington Spa General	arr	1 34	6 19
Solihull	,,	..	6 44
Birmingham (Snow Hill)	,,	2 5	6 55
Wolverhampton (Low Level)	,,	..	7 20

MEALS AND REFRESHMENTS SERVED AT EVERY SEAT
Supplementary Charges (for each single journey)

Between	LONDON (Paddington) 1st	2nd	LEAMINGTON SPA GENERAL 1st	2nd	SOLIHULL 1st	2nd	BIRMINGHAM (Snow Hill) 1st	2nd	WOLVERHAMPTON (Low Level) 1st	2nd
LEAMINGTON SPA GENERAL	8/-	4/-	–	–	2/-	1/-	2/-	1/-	3/-	1/6
SOLIHULL	10/-	5/-	2/-	1/-	–	–	2/-	1/-	2/6	1/-
BIRMINGHAM (Snow Hill) ..	10/-	5/-	2/6	1/-	2/-	1/-	–	–	2/-	1/-
WOLVERHAMPTON (L. Level)	10/-	5/-	3/-	1/6	2/6	1/-	2/-	1/-	–	–

The Supplementary Charge is payable in addition to the usual First and Second Class Fares applicable to the journey being made.

THE NUMBER OF PASSENGERS CARRIED IS LIMITED TO THE SEATING ACCOMMODATION AVAILABLE.

Seats can be reserved in advance at stations and usual agencies for journeys from and to all the stations shewn above. Subsequent reservations may be effected with the Pullman Car Conductor on the train if accommodation is available.

Pullman Car Tickets will only be issued subject to these conditions.

these, a service of Sunday Paddington expresses began the following day, 2 October 1910.

On 2 March 1914 the lines south of Wolverhampton came under the GWR's Birmingham Area Telephone Train Control system which directly connected five train control staff with over 130 passenger and goods installations. Primarily of benefit to goods operations, this system enabled these to interfere with passenger workings as little as possible. Through this, and the other improvements mentioned, the 1915 summer timetable boasted 13 Wolverhampton-Birmingham-Paddington-only expresses, nine of which had restaurant or tea cars; additional morning and evening expresses stopping at Bilston, Wednesbury and West Bromwich to save business travellers having to change trains at Snow Hill. By most of these trains, Wolverhampton was now only

2hr 24min from Paddington, the 12½ miles from Birmingham being reduced to only 19min, and even less from 1922.

The introduction of through booking from Wolverhampton Low Level, via the Southern Railway, to stations in Europe on 8 July 1929, finally recognised the important role the town was playing in the GWR's operations, as did the operation of its Automatic Train Control signalling on the lines running south of the Low Level from 7 October 1931. By 1932, in addition to London expresses, Wolverhampton was an important starting point for trains to Penzance and Weymouth as well as a stop for trains from Liverpool to Hastings and Portsmouth, from Manchester to Bournemouth West, and for the 'Cambrian Coast Express' to Aberystwyth.

After nationalisation, the basic pattern of former GWR services was retained, with additions. 'The Inter-City' Paddington-Wolverhampton express was introduced on 25 September 1950, and between 18 June and 23 September 1951 the 'William Shakespeare' ran from Wolverhampton to Paddington via Stratford-on-Avon, in connection with the Festival of Britain; this being one of five Festival trains, the first to be formed of the new BR Standard Mk 1 corridor coaches and dining cars.

The working of 'King' class locomotives north of Wolverhampton had long been prohibited by the GWR due to weight and clearance difficulties; but these were re-evaluated by British Railways (Western Region) on 13 April 1959 when No 6011 *King James I* was run light engine north of Wolverhampton on weight and clearance tests, and was found to be safe to work on this route. So, on 20 April, No 6024 *King Edward I* worked the 'Cambrian Coast Express' through Low Level station

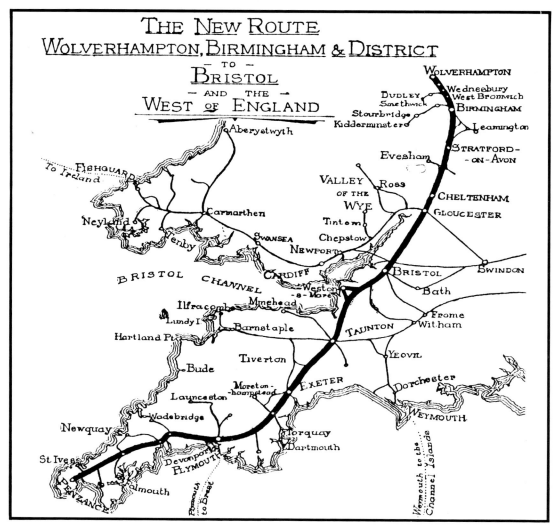

Above:
**'King' class No 6025 *King Henry III* takes the up
'Cambrian Coast Express' down the ex-OWW main line
on 18 May 1962.** *A. W. Smith*

Left:
**The GWR's new route between Wolverhampton, Bristol
and the West of England, which opened on 1 July 1908,
as it was presented to readers of the 1909 edition of the
*Official Guide to the Great Western Railway.***
Author's Collection

and on to Shrewsbury; with 'Kings' being used on
similar duties throughout the summer timetable in
1959 and each subsequent summer until their
official withdrawal in the autumn of 1962.

British Railways' Modernisation Plan, published
in January 1955, heralded the adoption of diesel
traction, and in April 1957 it was announced that it
was intended to build 'diesel-electric multi-car
deluxe trains to operate at high speed between
London and Wolverhampton (WR)'. These were the
'Blue Pullmans' and when introduced on 12 September 1960 they ran from a much busier Low Level
station, which had, from 2 November 1959, been
operating additional London services to compensate
for the almost withdrawn Euston service from the
High Level station pending electrification work.

The 'Birmingham Pullman' could maintain speeds
of 90mph, and regularly arrived ahead of schedule.
The eight-car train could seat 108 first-class
passengers, each of whom paid an 11/- supplement
to the ordinary fare, and 120 second-class passengers, who paid a 5/6d supplement; all of the seats
being bookable, Wolverhampton's allocation of
these being 18 in each class. The 'Birmingham
Pullman' set's movements rarely took it far from
the Paddington-Wolverhampton line except for
occasions when it required maintenance, or when, as
on Sunday 27 August 1961, it required turning after
receiving running repairs and had to travel to
Shrewsbury as the locally available triangular
junction at Oxley was out of use due to the switching
out of Oxley West signalbox on Sundays.

Further changes were made in 1962. On 24 July it

was announced that the service to Penzance, named
The Cornishman from 18 June 1951 onwards, would,
from 10 September, no longer run from Wolverhampton Low Level but would start from Sheffield
Midland, running via Derby and Birmingham New
Street to Bristol and Penzance. In later years this
would be extended to run from Bradford Forster
Square. It was also announced that on the same day
an existing Wolverhampton-Bournemouth service
would be given the name of the LMR's 'Pines
Express' and rescheduled to start from Manchester
as part of the West Coast main line electrification
scheme.

Then, on 14 August 1962, it was announced that
the new 'Western' diesel-hydraulics would replace
the ex-GWR 'King' class locomotives, the mainstay
of the Paddington expresses for 35 years, on
10 September. Crew training on these locomotives
had taken place throughout the period of the
summer timetable (11 June-16 September), when
D1004 *Western Crusader* had been allocated to
Stafford Road shed. This was used on the 6.50am
and 10.15am Wolverhampton-Stourbridge local services and their 07.55am and 11.50am return runs
(until 30 July); each afternoon D1004 also hauled the
4.53pm Wolverhampton-Chester service, working
the 9.45pm Chester-Paddington service back as far
as Wolverhampton. A fortnight later D1000 *Western
Enterprise*, D1002 *Western Explorer,* and D1005
Western Venturer, together with D1004, were
allocated to Oxley shed and began to run regularly
on the Wolverhampton to Paddington services,
working the 10.35am up and 4.10pm down trains
Mondays to Thursdays and taking an earlier turn on
Fridays and Saturdays.

Last 'King' specials were run from Wolverhampton on 8 and 9 September, the inaugural run of
D1000 *Western Enterprise* on the 10.35am Wolverhampton Low Level-Paddington service the following day being marred only by a faulty signal at
Wednesbury, which helped to make the train 20min
late arriving in London; possibly a good omen of
things to come. For, despite the Western Region's
hopes for these locomotives, there were both

reliability and availability problems with them in their early months of service on the Wolverhampton-Paddington services, resulting in a number of substitutions by steam locomotives, including, on at least three occasions, turns by officially withdrawn 'King' class engines in late 1962. For example, on 30 October No 6011 *King James I* worked the 9.35am Wolverhampton-Paddington service, deputising for a failed 'Western'; that 17 November No 6000 *King George V* worked the up 4.35pm 'Inter-City' and on 21 December *King James I* worked the Paddington-Wolverhampton leg of the 10.50am down service to Shrewsbury.

The Development of Goods Facilities and Services

As with its stations and lines in the Wolverhampton area, the GWR also inherited its goods facilities in the town. The earliest were those built around the Victoria Basin on the Birmingham Canal, near the High Level station. This basin was dug out as part of the work undertaken to construct the S&B in the 1848-49 period.

As opened by the S&B, on 12 November 1849, Victoria Basin's facilities were the canal arm, with a wooden trans-shipment shed erected over part of it. This was served by three sidings, which branched out from a single spur, leaving the S&B line at Stafford Road Junction; all standard gauge. Denied rail access to Birmingham via the LNWR-controlled Stour Valley line, the S&B had to be content to send any goods it received on south by the Birmingham Canal. Although this was leased by the LNWR, it did not object to the S&B using it, as this brought the LNWR some additional revenue; whereas opening

the Stour Valley line would have opened Birmingham up to a competing railway company.

In anticipation of the amalgamation of the S&B company with the GWR on 1 September 1854, the latter relaid the Victoria Basin branch, and some of its sidings, with mixed gauge rail; opening this officially, with the rest of its facilities in Wolverhampton, on 14 November 1854. With the S&B, the GWR also acquired the former's half share in the High Level station, electing to use the station's goods facilities, as described in the previous chapter. It installed its goods clerks in the former S&B Boardroom, above the arched entrance to the High Level station's carriage drive, and left the LNWR's goods operations out at the ex-GJR 'Wolverhampton' station at Wednesfield Heath.

Victoria Basin was of immense importance to the GWR at this time. It could not run through goods trains north of Wolverhampton due to the break of gauge, all such consignments needing to be transferred to narrow gauge wagons. Therefore, the GWR had converted Victoria Basin to function as a transfer station, the first such on the company's system. Until the autumn of 1859, this transfer station handled all goods from the south that were going on further north, and vice versa. It also received any goods from the town and outlying districts that were to go south; it only being similar loads destined northwards that were handled at the High Level goods station in Mill Street.

Below:
'King' class No 6020 *King Henry IV* waits with empty stock on the centre road at Low Level station, to add to, and to take over the 11.40 Birkenhead to Paddington service on Whit Monday, 11 June 1962. *Michael Mensing*

Above:

D1000 *Western Enterprise* **brings the stock of the inaugural 'Western'-hauled Wolverhampton express, the 10.35 Wolverhampton-Paddington service, into Low Level station on 10 September 1962. Delays made it 20min late arriving in London.** *Ned Williams Collection*

Left:

D1005 *Western Venturer* **waits at Wolverhampton Low Level with additional coaches to reinforce and take over the up 'Cambrian Coast Express' on 27 August 1962, just before the 'Westerns' took over all workings between Low Level and Paddington from 10 September 1962.** *Michael Mensing*

Clearly, the unholy alliance between the GWR and the LNWR over use of the High Level station's goods facilities could not go on forever. Indeed, it is clear that the GWR was acutely aware of this; the main reason it gave for eventually selling the half share in the station to the LNWR for £65,000 on 1 March 1859 being that its new goods station, on the Victoria Basin site, would be ready that autumn, which it was. This comprised a wooden shed, which had somewhat narrow platforms either side of the main cart roadway and was equipped with fixed, hand-operated cranes; the platforms being connected by a hand-operated lifting bridge. It could deal with about 40 trucks at one time, and was officially designated the 'Wolverhampton Town Goods Station', but quickly became known by the name of the road from which its cart roadway was entered; Herbert Street Goods. Surmounting the goods shed, at the Herbert Street end, was a three-storey brick-built warehouse, used for the storage of grain and sugar, and a range of small-roomed offices.

The GWR's other goods facilities in Wolverhampton were built by the OWW, at the end of a branch which left its line at Stow Heath, just past Priestfield station. This comprised a large rectangular four-bay timber-framed and timber-clad shed for the trans-shipment of goods between rail and road vehicles, with an adjoining basin on the Birmingham Canal, situated on the other side of the LNWR's Stour Valley line, next to the Shrubbery ironworks. Hence its name: Shrubbery Basin. Road access to the goods shed was off Lower Walsall Street, but it became known as Walsall Street Goods, opening in October 1855. These facilities were acquired by the GWR upon its amalgamation with the WM on 1 August 1863.

Southbound GWR goods trains were run on the broad gauge, evinced by the derailment of 0-6-0 locomotive *Ariadne* en route to London on 5 January 1861. There were four such broad gauge goods trains in each direction daily; running until the end of the broad gauge to Birmingham on 1 April 1869.

Once established, the GWR built up its goods traffic in Wolverhampton. In 1890 it dealt with a total weight of goods just in excess of 180,000 tons, but by the 1930s this had almost doubled to 350,000 tons annually, involving the handling of over 130 loaded trucks inwards, and 110 outwards daily. In 1929, the GWR also named 75 of its long-distance night express goods services, 14 of which operated to or from Wolverhampton, from such destinations as Basingstoke, Bristol, Manchester, Paddington, Westbury, West Drayton, Birkenhead and Crewe.

Yet, despite the laying of more sidings at Herbert Street, the GWR's goods facilities in Wolverhampton were at capacity. Walsall Street had been improved in the spring of 1923, including new lifts costing £20,000: but something more radical was required. Plans centred around improvements to Herbert Street. Under the Government's Loans & Guarantees Act (1929), devised to encourage large capital works projects to relieve unemployment, the GWR proposed a 16-scheme plan, No 8 of which was for the reconstruction of Herbert Street Goods. The main contracts were let by April 1930, and the new goods station opened in November 1931. The reconstruction involved the demolition of the old goods shed and the complete remodelling and extension of the whole of the goods station over an increased area made available by filling in Victoria Basin and the demolition of buildings previously occupied by Messrs Danks & Walker, plus the closing of parts of Southampton, Herbert, Faulkner and Littles Streets and the clearance of slum housing contained therein. Only the three-storey warehouse remained from the original buildings; the new goods shed having a total area of 68,000sq ft and holding nearly 80 wagons. It had two platforms, 500ft long and 12ft and 30ft wide respectively, connected in the centre by a hand-operated balancing bridge, and a roof clearance of 21ft. A mileage yard holding 300 trucks, an increase of 100 over the old station, was built on the site of the slum housing. Extensive loading and unloading pens for livestock were also provided on the other side of the Cannock Road, part of these being covered; and the goods station had two entrances, one from Littles Lane and one from Great Western Street, both with weighbridges.

Reconstructing Herbert Street Goods coincided with a rationalisation of the GWR's trans-shipment centres, involving the end of trans-shipments locally at Cradley and Dudley. This was an obvious success, as the bridge carrying the Herbert Street branch over the Cannock Road had to be strengthened in May 1936. The facilities described served the GWR and British Railways (Western Region) for the next 30 years or so unaltered, save for the installation of Robotug automatic guided goods handling equipment at Herbert Street in September 1960; the first station to be so equipped in the country. At that time, 180 were employed at Herbert Street, which handled 180 tons of goods daily; 120 motor wagons bringing in 240 tons of goods each day from the area within a 10-mile radius of Wolverhampton. Herbert Street was also the star of the 9-14 April 1962 Birmingham Division 'Western Railway Week' events when special DMU services ran into there from Snow Hill, for a 2s 6d fare!

Right:
The ex-OWW goods shed at Walsall Street was opened in October 1855, and acquired by the GWR upon amalgamation with the WM Railway on 1 August 1863. The original timber buildings are seen here on 14 June 1964. *Eric Hamilton Collection*

Below:
The interior of the new goods shed in the rebuilt Herbert Street goods depot upon opening in 1930. The building on the left is the warehouse remaining from the old depot. *Wolverhampton Library*

4: Stafford Road Locomotive Works 1849-1964

Without Stafford Road Locomotive works, usually referred to as Stafford Road works or just 'Stafford Road', Wolverhampton's claim to be a rail centre would rest solely upon it having had two main stations and a bit of trouble over its railways in the 1840s and 1850s. For almost 50 years, this establishment produced some of the most distinctive locomotives and characters to serve the GWR; and for a further 60 years continued to maintain the motive power of its busiest operating division.

The Origins and Establishment of Stafford Road Works

As with so much that was 'railway' about Wolverhampton, Stafford Road works had its origins in the Shrewsbury & Birmingham Railway (S&B). By 1847 this company was already resigned to not reaching Birmingham by its own line, and had set about making its headquarters at Wolverhampton, including some form of locomotive accommodation and repair facility. This would not be the first such establishment in the town, for, as we have seen, the Grand Junction Railway repaired locomotives in the workshops and smithies associated with its station at Wednesfield Heath.

In its choice of site the S&B was limited to one within easy access of its line, which meant to the northwest, and probably to one by the road leading to Stafford, whose course the S&B's line followed and crossed as it approached the town. Wolverhampton's rapid growth at this time (13,500 additional inhabitants in the 1840s alone), further limited the S&B's choice. Along the Stafford Road the town was built up to Fox's Lane, and a ¼-mile on from this, at Gosbrook, an auxiliary gasworks was being built, leaving a prime site ready for infilling, which the S&B duly purchased.

Construction of the locomotive works did not begin before 1849, as, early that year, the S&B's minutes record that: 'It was very desirable forthwith to erect engine and carriage repair shops', and it was ordered that 'Mr (Edward) Banks (the S&B's Architect and Surveyor) prepare plans for the necessary buildings to be erected on the land', which he did. Later in the year the minutes noted that the building contractor was: 'to erect the shops on

Below:
Stafford Road Locomotive works, 1852.

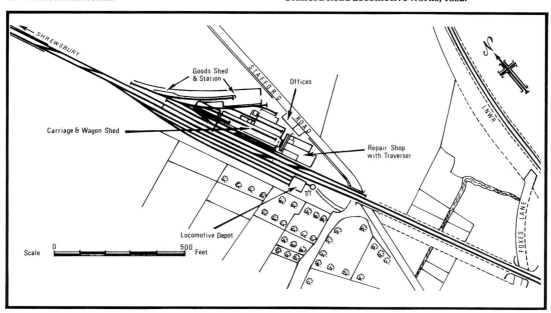

69

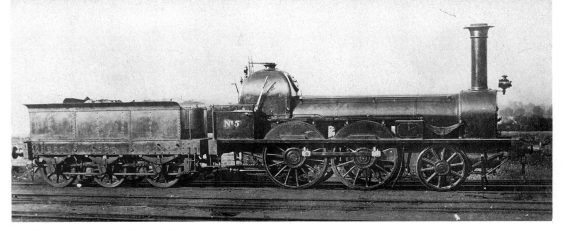

condition of a penalty clause of £300 per week if not completed by 4 August', which he refused to accept; and so it wasn't until 20 July that he was: 'directed to commence at once the erection of the workshops from the plans prepared by Mr Banks and at the schedule of prices agreed'.

The work was completed around the time of the S&B's opening on 12 November 1849. This first development on the site was built between the west side of Stafford Road and the main S&B line, with a goods station on the other side of this. These buildings comprised a locomotive shed, carriage and wagon shed, repair shop, with traverser, a goods shed, and offices fronting to Stafford Road; the latter being completed around 1852. The layout of the original buildings shown on page 69 which is based upon an 1852 survey of Wolverhampton.

Where these first shops were built the land rises up to Dunstall Hill. This has led some to refer to this part of Stafford Road works as 'The High Level'. Owing to the confusion this inevitably brings with Wolverhampton's station of the same name, use of this term will be avoided, preference being given to the term 'the ex-S&B shops'.

Although the S&B owned all 23 of the locomotives used on its line they were operated initially by a locomotive contractor, Johnson & Kinder of Bromsgrove, with William Marlow as Locomotive Superintendent at Wolverhampton. By late 1852 the S&B was dissatisfied with Johnson & Kinder's work and appointed the Hon Edmund Petre as an Inspector to supervise their activities. This move went down well, and, together with a plan to pool the locomotives of the S&B with those of the adjoining Shrewsbury & Chester Railway (S&C), it forced Johnson & Kinder to end their contract in April 1853, leaving Petre to control both companies' stock.

He remained at Wolverhampton for a year, during which time the repair shops at Stafford Road rebuilt their first locomotives; S&B Nos 1, 2, 4 and 5, as 0-4-2 tender goods engines, with only the (shortened) boilers remaining from the originals. Petre left in April 1854 to take up a similar post on the North British Railway, and was succeeded by Joseph

Armstrong, who had been Locomotive Superintendent of the S&C at its works at Saltney near Chester since 1852.

The Start of Locomotive Building at Stafford Road Works

With the amalgamation of the S&B and S&C with the GWR from 1 September 1854, the latter acquired control of both companies' assets, including Stafford Road works. Initially, these narrow gauge lines were effectively isolated by gauge differences from the GWR's main locomotive works at Swindon. It therefore made sense to recognise this by the creation of a separate locomotive Northern Division, and to centralise all locomotive repair operations somewhere within this. Thus on 12 October 1854 the GWR's Locomotive Superintendent, one Daniel Gooch, told the Board that he 'considered that it would be most economical and serviceable to retain all the buildings and machinery at the Stafford Road station near Wolverhampton, and adapt them for both broad and narrow gauge purposes, as the only engine repairing establishment in the Northern Division up to and including Birmingham'.

Gooch also submitted the plans of the present shops at Wolverhampton, noting what alterations they required: 'The Carriage & Wagon depot to be entirely removed to Saltney, and the premises located at the Stafford Road to be converted for the Locomotive Department; machinery to be brought from Shrewsbury and placed in the Stafford Road station, excepting such as adapted and required for wagon purposes.' Gooch added that 'some additional steam shed room would be found necessary at Wolverhampton'; that it would be best to concentrate the Northern Division stores in the present building at Wolverhampton, which 'was adequate and available for the purpose', and that: 'it would be desirable to place the superintendence and charge of the Department between Birmingham and the North under Mr (Joseph) Armstrong'.

Thus began a long association between the Armstrong family and Stafford Road works, and a lengthy period of conversion of the repair shops into a locomotive works that would only see 20 new engines produced there in the next 10 years. Joseph Armstrong also brought his brother George with him from the S&C, and in October 1855 took on one William Dean as a pupil.

Gooch originally intended to carry out all narrow gauge locomotive building and substantial repairs at Swindon, engines being carried there on special broad gauge trucks. May 1855 saw the first narrow gauge locomotives, 12 0-6-0 goods engines, built at Swindon to Gooch's design; but the impracticality of this idea soon became apparent and the policy was reversed, requiring the extensive rearrangement of Stafford Road works for locomotive production. This took the better part of 10 years.

Late in 1858, with Herbert Street goods station nearing completion, plans were made for the extension of the facilities at Stafford Road. Once Herbert Street was opened, the goods station adjoining the works could be cleared. On this a boiler shop was built, together with an iron foundry, and, next to the road, a Mechanics Institute, on the site of a former Turnpike Trust tollhouse. A new running shed was also built near to the end of Oxley viaduct, enabling the original shed in the ex-S&B works to be converted into an erecting shop with a wheel shop to one side of it. This was connected via a traverser to a wide shop which had been used for running maintenance and general locomotive repairs. Two of the roads in this were retained for locomotive building, the remainder being taken up and the space created being used as a machine shop. A fitting shop was built over the traverser pit, and a patternmakers' shop was situated over a boiler and engine house. The former large goods shed, alongside the Stafford Road Junction-Cannock Road Junction line, was converted to or replaced by a forge and smithy, which included a tyre furnace.

By 1859 these alterations and extensions were far enough advanced for Joseph Armstrong to begin to build engines to his own design. Accordingly, that September Stafford Road works built its first completely new locomotives, the 2-2-2 express singles Nos 7 and 8, which took the numbers of two

ex-S&C locomotives withdrawn at the same time. As with all of Armstrong's subsequent designs, these engines were characterised by clean lines and a design simplicity which marked quite a departure from Gooch's essentially 'narrowed' broad gauge locomotives.

The Development of Stafford Road Works

Locomotive building having commenced at Stafford Road, it hardly proceeded apace. Another 2-2-2 express locomotive, No 30, was built in March 1860, but was not followed until No 110 was built in June 1862. Why the delay? The difficulty lay in the fact that the works was being asked to perform the two different functions of locomotive construction and maintenance. Most of its capacity to build locomotives was being taken up with repairs to a growing narrow gauge stock, much of it acquired from absorbed companies, and originating from small orders placed with different builders, some of whom no longer existed. Therefore spares had often to be made.

Matters came to a head when the West Midland Railway amalgamated with the GWR in August 1863. This brought the narrow gauge locomotive stock up to 301; only 57 built by the GWR (44 at Swindon, nine at Wolverhampton, and four at Worcester). Some light repairs (and later rebuilds) were undertaken at the ex-OWW locomotive works at Worcester, but the heavier work still came to Stafford Road. A further expansion of the works therefore became a priority.

Extending the existing works around the ex-S&B shops was complicated by the excavation this would

require into the sandstone forming Dunstall Hill and the landowner so affected was not keen on the idea. Over the Stafford Road was the broad gauge running shed (described in Chapter 3) in the Lower Yard. With the rundown in broad gauge services in Wolverhampton, some of this shed's capacity had become vacant. There was also additional spare land adjacent to this shed.

Therefore, some of the ex-S&B shops were duplicated in the Lower Yard; the space between the broad gauge running shed and stores building making a site for new erecting, fitting and machine shops, plus a smithy. The broad gauge shed itself later became a tender shop. To connect what was

Below:
Stafford Road Locomotive works, 1883.

Bottom:
Built at Stafford Road works-1. '111' class No 1009 was built in August 1866, one of 20 such locomotives built at Wolverhampton between 1863 and 1887. They were the first class of 2-4-0s to be designed by Joseph Armstrong, and were used on secondary services. No 1009 was withdrawn in January 1904. *LPC*

now a split site, a wide footbridge was built over the Stafford Road to give the ex-S&B shops direct access to the stores in the Lower Yard. These changes are summarised in a diagram, which is based upon an 1886 OS map. Whilst this work was being undertaken at Wolverhampton, there were other changes afoot at Swindon.

George Armstrong and Stafford Road Works

Daniel Gooch retired as the GWR's Locomotive Superintendent in the summer of 1864, but he was persuaded to remain as the company's Chairman. The GWR's Carriage and Wagon Superintendent also retired at the same time and the Directors appointed Joseph Armstrong to succeed to both positions; beginning a tradition in such promotions. He left his brother George in charge at Stafford Road, and William Dean as his Assistant and Works Manager, having been responsible for the building of only 28 locomotives there. Over the ensuing 33 years George Armstrong would add a six in front of this, developing his own high standards and methods at Stafford Road.

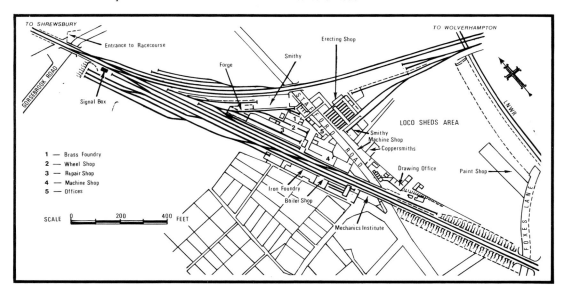

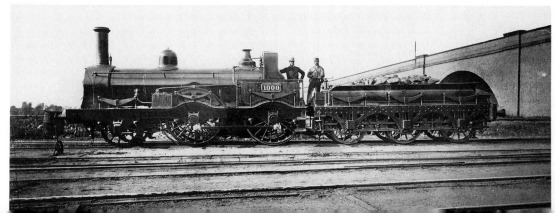

Space does not permit a detailed consideration of the locomotives built at Wolverhampton; to do this justice would require a book in its own right. But an insight into what went on there can be gained through an understanding of what George Armstrong was trying to achieve. The main problem facing him has already been mentioned: the diversity of locomotives the GWR had acquired. By 1864, this totalled some 180 engines, plus 154 others, built mostly to Gooch or Joseph Armstrong designs by the GWR, or Beyer Peacock of Manchester. George Armstrong's solution was to implement a major policy of locomotive rebuilding, to be undertaken on each locomotive when major repairs became necessary; in tandem with the building of new locomotives using the same components.

In this way, non-standard components were gradually replaced with standard ones, particular attention being paid to boilers, cylinders and motions. The nature of the rebuilds instigated under this policy varied considerably; from scrapping the older engine and replacing it with a new one, through extensive alterations, which may only retain a few parts of the original (part of the frame, the buffer bar, splasher, etc), to something as 'minor' as a boiler and firebox replacement. Yet, whilst all of this was aimed at standardisation, it was not done with any want of individuality.

Quite quickly George Armstrong developed what has become known as the 'Wolverhampton style'.

More than mere livery diferences, this manifested itself in a number of ways: narrow chimneys with smaller diameter, more rounded rolled copper tops than those fitted at Swindon; flat or dished smokebox doors, and individual designs for splashers, wheel boxes and side platforms. Even more noticeable were the Wolverhampton boilers, each with a tall brass dome placed on the middle of three rings, and fed by a barrel clackbox, most topped by raised firebox casings and characteristic brass safety valve covers. Very apparent to drivers was the Armstrong cab, or rather the lack of it. As ex-drivers themselves, neither Joseph nor George saw the need to provide anything more than they had enjoyed: a weatherboard with two circular windows in it. All of this was then finished off with a highly individual livery.

The origins of the 'Wolverhampton livery' lay in the OWW, whose deep blue-green colour was retained for painting the locomotive and tender bodywork. Boiler bands and body panels were lined in black edged in white, the frames, wheels and coupling rods were painted a dark purple-brown, the chimney and smokebox were painted black, and the buffer beams were painted red and lined in black. Until the adoption of cast numberplates by the GWR in 1876, the locomotive number was painted on in gold with black shading, and beyond this date tenders continued to have their locomotive's number painted on the frame. Minor variations in this livery were introduced in 1866 and 1888, but it remained

Right:
Built at Stafford Road works-2. '1016' class 0-6-0ST No 1070 was built at Wolverhampton in July 1871 to a Joseph Armstrong design. The 60 engines of this class typify the GWR's policy of locomotive rebuilding. No 1070 worked as a saddle tank for 52 years before receiving pannier tanks in August 1923 and working until August 1932. It is seen here about 1880. *LPC*

Below:
Rebuilt at Stafford Road works-1. GWR No 184 began as OWW No 23, built by E. B. Wilson & Co in 1853. It was rebuilt at Wolverhampton in February 1871 and is seen here around 1880 after receiving a cab and cast numberplate. No 184 was withdrawn in October 1899. *LPC*

virtually unaltered until 1902, when 'Swindon' livery was adopted. Completing the livery was the practice of patterning the top coat of varnish each locomotive received to produce the rough honeycombed/ diamond pattern effect that can be seen in photographs taken of freshly outshopped Wolverhampton engines. One final peculiarity was the Stafford Road practice of setting locomotive valves to equal port openings, front and back. Contemporary accounts attest to the superior pulling and running power that this practice gave, particularly with 7ft single passenger express locomotives.

Progressively, all of the older types of locomotive in the Northern Division were either replaced or rebuilt; attention also being turned to some of the earlier Swindon and Wolverhampton-built engines. Only one locomotive escaped this treatment, ex-S&C No 14. It has been suggested that this was George Armstrong's favourite from his S&C driving days. In any case it was kept, minus its tender, on two short lengths of bridge rail between two of the radial roads in Stafford Road's No 2 running shed where it

stood, apart from being used for practice by apprentices from the paint shop, until it was cut up on 21 January 1920 for 'being in the way'!

George Armstrong's freedom to pursue his own policies at Stafford Road evolved for a variety of reasons. Wolverhampton's locomotive building was

Above:
Built at Stafford Road works-3. Stafford Road did not only build engines for use in the GWR's Northern Division. No 643, one of 12 '633' Class 0-6-0Ts, was built as shown in March 1872, with condensing apparatus for use over the Metropolitan line in London. It was withdrawn in February 1934. *LPC*

Below:
S&C No 14 was said to be George Armstrong's favourite from his S&C driving days. Whatever the case, it survived his rebuilding policy and was stored on two short lengths of bridge rail in Stafford Road No 2 shed until it was cut up on 21 January 1920 for 'being in the way'. *LPC*

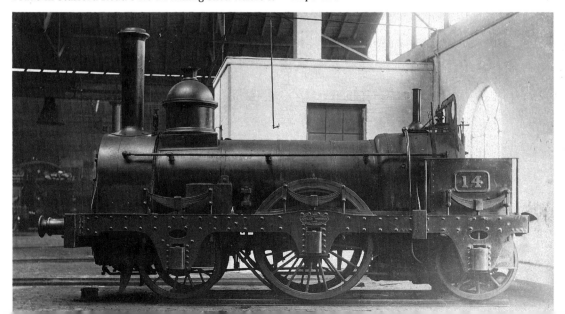

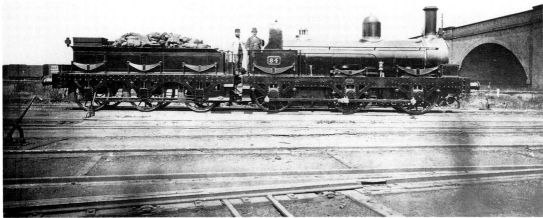

Top:
Built at Stafford Road works-4. '517' Class No 1164 was one of the second group of this large class to be built, most of which had side rather than saddle tanks. No 1164 is shown new from the works in the Lower Yard at Stafford Road in March 1876. Note the patterned finish on the tank sides and the painted number. From 1876 the GWR began to use cast numberplates.
Bucknall Collection/Ian Allan Library

Above:
Rebuilt at Stafford Road works-2. Stafford Road also rebuilt engines orginally built at Swindon, which is where '79' Class No 84 was made in 1857. It was 'renewed' at Wolverhampton in February 1877, where it is seen in the Lower Yard area. *LPC*

nominally under the charge of Swindon, where he was fortunate in only being 'governed' by two men in his entire period at Stafford Road: his brother Joseph, until his death in 1877, and Joseph's successor, William Dean, who until June 1868 had been George Armstrong's Works Manager at Wolverhampton. Dean had been called to Swindon as Joseph Armstrong's No 2, taking with him his

Confidential Clerk, W. H. Stainer, whose son, W. A., also worked on the railway. Neither man at Swindon was therefore inclined to argue with George Armstrong, who was by all accounts not a man to be argued with.

For all his individuality, George Armstrong nonetheless did what was required of him, and to a far higher standard than any but himself would have expected. He was also a very fair and generous man; turning Stafford Road into possibly the most important training ground for railway engineers in the country. At the heart of what was then the GWR's busiest running centre, this relatively small works offered a down-to-earth and sharply focused practical experience, as the need to keep as much of Wolverhampton's motive power running as possible dominated the works activities.

At its heyday under George Armstrong, the scene around Stafford Road works was captured by the author of an irreverent guide to Wolverhampton, published in 1884:

'The various sheds are built on either side of the road, whilst the large building a little to the left with steps from the far end and farthest from the road, which have the appearance of a 'slantingdicular' tunnel is the Institute which contains Lending Library, News Room, Bagatelle and Billiards Boards, and all the necessary drawings &c, incident to the proper training of an engineer. A little lower down, behind the clock, are the main offices, and here some dozens of clerks intersperse their scribblings in huge leather bound books by sundry human weaknesses in the usual approved style. The workmen employed here number some 3,000 souls, and any stranger passing down here about 1.0pm must have a very righteous soul indeed, if he can bear the running fire of compliments showered upon him by begreased "sheddies" without violating the injunction "Swear not at all". The hour of commencing work is early and has to be kept so prompt that men have been paid to call them to time.'

Twenty-three years later, a visit to Stafford Road made by the University of Birmingham Engineering Society (on 8 February 1907), has preserved a description of the layout and functioning of the works immediately prior to the end of locomotive building there:

'We were first taken into the boiler-erecting shop, where some half-dozen boilers were in various stages of construction. On one of these the throttle valve and lever were in position and connected up. The valve and lever being, of course, at opposite ends of the boiler, those who were examining the lever and seeing if it would work could not see if the valve was fitted. The lever worked, and with disastrous results, the valve inspector having his fingers rather severely squeezed. A liberal application of water and sal volatile, however, enabled him to see the other shops. The second shop visited was one in which the parts of boilers and fireboxes were made. Here, plate benders and pneumatic chippers and riveters were seen at work. We watched a rivet made in a firebox by a hand pneumatic riveter, a considerable length of metal being hammered down to form a well-shaped rivet-head in about three minutes. This shop also contained a riveter capable of dealing with steel rivets up to one inch in diameter, the head being completed in two blows, it was steam driven.

'The iron foundry was next seen. This was only a small shop, as there is not much cast-iron on locomotive work. The pattern shop besides two or three lathes and band and circular saws, contained a machine which was a combined driller and slotter, the drilling spindle and slotting ram being side by side. The machine

shops now engaged our attention. The first contained a multitude of small machines of all kinds, and was used for the general locomotive work. An automatic was noticed turning out some rather large set-pins, and a grinding machine was engaged in finishing the piston rods. The pistons are screwed on to the rods, which are then riveted over. The coupling rod bushes are made solid, though, of course, the connecting rod brasses are in halves. The second shop was employed in wheel turning. All sizes were being machined, both on the rim and in the bore, the largest being a pair each eight feet in diameter.

'In the yard at the end of this shop four burly smiths were hammering away on the tyre of a wheel, which had just been shrunk on the wheel itself, to secure the key which prevents the tyre from working off sideways. Here in the open were two large steam hammers, which were engaged in forging frames. The frames are not cut out from plates, but are forged, on account of the waste metal which the former method entails. The smithy proper was then entered. The steam hammers are arranged down the centre with hearths on either side. The wheels are made here. The arms of a wheel are all forged separately, each having a portion of the rim and the boss made with it. These are then welded together at the boss, and piece is welded in between each arm to complete the rim.

'The brass foundry came next, and we found that they were nearly ready to pour, so we waited so see this, the time being occupied in examining the intricate mould for an injector. The shop where new engines are built was the next seen. This is only a small shop, with room for about four engines. The engines are built in stages, and when one stage is completed the partially built engine is moved on to the place where the next stage is proceeded with. Thus each portion of the shop has its own work. The repairing shop itself has room for about a dozen engines, the rails and pits being on either side, while the centre is given up to miscellaneous spare parts. The engines were in various states of decay, some, having only come in for small repairs, looked nearly new, whereas others seemed decrepit enough to require rebuilding. In the small drawing office we were shown, among other things, a finished drawing of a tank engine, and a partially finished one of a snow plough.

'In a shed the valve setter was at work. He explained to us that he set the valves so that they gave equal port opening, the leads being unequal with the larger at the front end. The painting shop, which we entered next, contained nine engines. It is run on a fortnightly system, the complete painting system taking a fortnight. The visit ended at the motor-car shed, where steam

Above:
Built at Stafford Road works-5. An example of the final form of the '517' class 0-4-2Ts. No 1423 was built at Wolverhampton in May 1877 and is seen here when fitted with a Swindon style cab, but whilst retaining its Wolverhampton bunker. No 1423 was withdrawn in February 1930. *LPC*

Right:
Before: **GWR No 189 began as OWW No 41, built by E. B. Wilson & Co in 1855, and is seen here in unrebuilt condition, save for the addition of a GWR cast numberplate.** *LPC*

motors were being constructed and repaired. The engines have outside cylinders, and the valves are operated by Walschaert's gear. The shops are driven by locomotive engines used as stationaries, and the steam is generated in locomotive boilers.'

George Armstrong retired in 1897 at the age of 75. In his 33 years in charge at Stafford Road the works had built 626 new locomotives, and rebuilt a further 513, mostly 0-6-0 saddle tanks and 0-4-2 tank engines. Sadly, there was no Armstrong to replace him; young Joe Armstrong, Joseph's son, and George Armstrong's Works Manager, having been run down and killed by a locomotive at the works on 1 January 1888. And so W. H. Waister, the Works Manager when George Armstrong retired, succeeded him, but this was only a stopgap appointment, J. A. Robinson (the elder brother of the Great Central Railway's Chief Mechanical Engineer J. G. Robinson) being appointed as Northern Division Locomotive Superintendent later in 1897.

The End of Locomotive Building at Stafford Road Works

Stafford Road's years of independence could be said to have been numbered from the extension of mixed gauge track as far as Swindon in February 1872. That locomotive building continued there for as long as it did speaks more of George Armstrong's independence, and the want of reorganisation at Swindon, than it does of anything else. By the 1890s, both works were badly in need of extension and modernisation. G. J. Churchward (William Dean's Assistant and eventual successor) and others recognised the coming need for locomotive developments, and the massive programme of locomotive building that would result from this. Unfortunately, neither Swindon nor Stafford Road were equipped to cope with such demands.

Around 1890, a scheme was devised to extend Stafford Road by excavating the sandstone of Dunstall Hill down to the level of the ex-S&B shops, and to use the excavated material to build up the hill's lower slopes to form an extensive plateau on which to build an up-to-date works. Its success depended upon the GWR being able to acquire the land this would require at reasonable cost. Ironically, the company had sold off this very same land as surplus to requirements some years previously. There was also opposition to the scheme from local landowners and residents. Negotiations to buy the land broke down over the price, and the scheme was shelved.

About this time, the GWR toyed with various ideas for the reorganisation of its locomotive building. One of these would have seen Stafford Road becoming the principal locomotive works, with Swindon being turned over to the manufacture of carriages and wagons. Unfortunately, land was more readily available at Swindon, and the GWR Board was persuaded to authorise the building of a new erecting shop there in June 1900. This became A shop, and began operating in May 1904. Later in 1900, the Stafford Road scheme was revived. Excavations began into Dunstall Hill, and later contractors were engaged, a sufficient area for the erection of a modern works being formed behind the ex-S&B shops by 1905. Plans and estimates for this were prepared, but a slump in traffic and receipts caused the scheme to be shelved again.

Meanwhile, locomotive building was continuing at Stafford Road, with the remainder of a large order for 160 0-6-0 saddle tank engines, which was completed in 1905. That same year Stafford Road was called upon to build 10 of the Churchward-designed 2-6-2 tank locomotives of the '3101' class, which appeared between July 1905 and June 1906. As with all other locomotives built at Wolverhampton, these were erected in the two-road 'new' engine shop at Stafford Road. This comprised two parallel pits, on one of which the locomotive's frames,

complete with cylinders, would be completed. The locomotive's boiler would be built in the boiler shop, and brought into the engine shop by means of the traverser, being lifted into place by means of a fixed overhead crane. The locomotive was then 'wheeled', and readied for delivery. Unfortunately, the 2-6-2 tanks were longer and heavier than the 0-6-0s and 0-4-2s for which the engine shop at Stafford Road had been laid out, even with their buffers removed. Therefore, a new route out of the shop was formed via the adjoining wheel shop. A temporary track, with sharp reverse curvatures and widened gauge, was laid over the traverser pit. To negotiate these,

Below:
After: No 186 was a sister engine to No 189 and was rebuilt to this form at Wolverhampton in December 1877. This is an excellent example of both Wolverhampton rebuilding and of 'Wolverhampton Style'. Only the front end of the frame and the splashers are said to have survived from the original locomotive. *LPC*

Bottom:
Rebuilt at Stafford Road works-3. 'Queen' class No 1116 is a good example of a later Wolverhampton rebuild of a Swindon locomotive, being rebuilt in August 1885 and seen here in the Lower Yard at Stafford Road. No 1116 was the only one of its class to retain open splashers after rebuilding. *LPC*

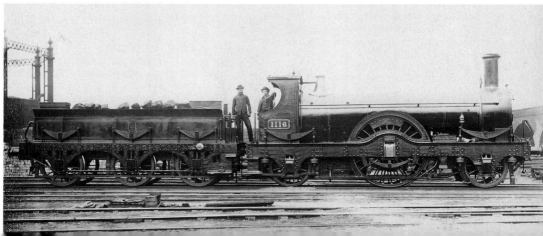

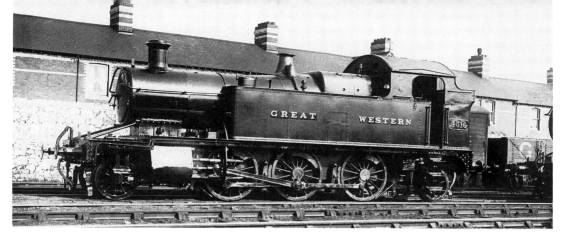

the locomotive's pony trucks were removed, thus
making them into 0-6-0s; and these emasculated
2-6-2s were then moved slowly, by a gang of men
with pinch bars, to a point where they could be
attached to the works shunting engine and pulled
clear of the curves. Once on the straight, the pony
trucks were reattached, and the newly restored
engines were pulled into the daylight, via a hole
knocked in the end of the wheel shop!

The building of these 2-6-2Ts highlighted Stafford
Road's inadquate capacity to cope with larger
locomotive designs, which was the form most future
construction would take. Consequently, after completing an order for a further 20 such locomotives no
more orders were placed at Stafford Road, the GWR
opting to concentrate all subsequent locomotive
building at Swindon. The last engine built at
Stafford Road was therefore 2-6-2T No 2180, which
was extricated from the new engine shop in April
1908, and renumbered as No 4519 in December 1912.

Since 1853, Stafford Road works had built 880 new
locomotives of which the greater proportion were
0-6-0s (528) or 0-4-2s (203), and all but 23 were tank
engines, predominantly saddle tanks. In addition the
works had rebuilt 575 locomotives, making a grand
total of 1,455.

Repairs and Delayed Development

George Armstrong's retirement in 1897 allowed his
eventual successor, J. A. Robinson, to set about
reorganising some aspects of Stafford Road works.
One that quickly came under his attention was the
training given to young men in the works. The
excellent opportunity for learning about locomotive
engineering that Stafford Road offered has already
been mentioned, but under George Armstrong this
had only been extended to 'pupils', identified
high-fliers destined for responsible positions in the
GWR's hierarchy. Apprentices had fared less well,
spending five years being trained, but having to take
pot-luck over which shop they began in, or how long
they would have to wait to move on to another shop.

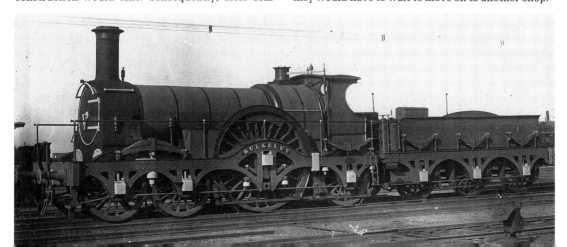

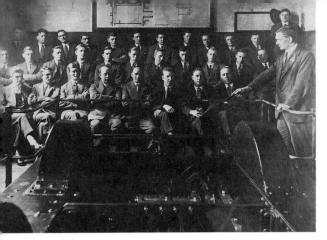

Left:
**Enginemen under model instruction at Stafford Road
works. Is that J. A. Robinson wielding the pointer?
Wake up at the back there!** *Ned Williams Collection*

Bottom:
**The basis for the Stafford Road model. Ex-OWW No 34
and GWR No 252 rebuilt at Wolverhampton in
November 1873. Withdrawn in August 1904, it served
Stafford Road works for a further 45 years at least.** *LPC*

Right:
**A wider view of the construction work on the new
erecting shop at Stafford Road works in 1931. The
wheels and tyres in the foreground are from
locomotives undergoing repair at the time.**
British Rail/OPC EO/543

Below right:
**Almost there. Bricking up the ends of the new erecting
shop at Stafford Road works in 1932. An SLS tour of the
works on 24 April 1932 noted locomotives undergoing
repair in this shop.** *British Rail/OPC EO/574*

Bottom right:
**Inside the new erecting shop at Stafford Road works in
July 1932, when the official GWR publicity photographs
were taken of the completed development there.**
Modern Transport

Robinson changed all this. He abolished the two
grades of trainee, instituting a five-year course with
planned progress through the various shops.
Additional courses were required to be taken at the
local Technical College in the winter, and greater use
was made of the works Mechanics Institute. Here, in
1910, Robinson installed an Engineman's Instruc-
tional Model comprising the leading and driving
wheels plus cylinders and motion, from ex-OWW
six-coupled goods locomotive No 252, withdrawn in
August 1904. Employing cut-away sections, the
model could be turned using a hand wheel to allow
the respective movements of the various components to be studied at close quarters, and in
comparative safety!

Of course, absent from any training received at
Stafford Road, from 1908 onwards, was any
practical experience in locomotive construction.
From then the works only undertook the repair and
overhaul of the kinds of locomotive that it had
formerly built, up to but excluding anything
necessitating the removal of the boiler, which had to
be dealt with at Swindon. Former skills stagnated,
and there was little investment in the works, save
for improvements to the Mechanics Institute to
install a concert and meeting hall, and to enlarge the
Mess Room; both commenced in November 1923.

The Redevelopment of Stafford
Road Works 1929-1932

Keenest of all the railway companies to take
advantage of money made available for the relief of
unemployment under the Government's Loans &
Guarantees (1929) Act, the GWR assembled a
package of capital schemes totalling £4.5 million
and employing 200,000 man-months. In order to get
this together so quickly it dusted off and revised
some abandoned schemes, including the reconstruction and modernisation of Stafford Road
works. This package was approved and building
began at the works on 5 November 1929, on the site
behind the ex-S&B shops partly prepared in 1905.
The main new building to be constructed was an

erecting shop, work progressing on the site throughout 1930 and 1931.

In April 1932, the *GWR Magazine* listed eight contracts placed with machine tool manufacturers for equipping the new shops. Unfortunately, this is misleading as to when the new erecting shop came into use as an SLS visit to Stafford Road on 24 April 1932 described the new buildings as in operation and local recollections are such that they were used *before* they were roofed. Either way, publicity for the opening of the new facilities appeared in the first week of August 1932 from when attention could be paid to reorganising the older parts of the works, which was completed in late 1933.

The main erecting shop was 450ft long by 196ft wide and consisted of three bays; two forming the erecting shop itself, the third the machine and wheel shop. Engines came in at the south end of the shop where the necessary stripping was carried out, and, in the case of a general repair, where the boiler was removed from the frame and sent directly to the boiler shop in the Lower Yard where a special track, powered by an electric capstan, had been laid for this purpose. Any item stripped from locomotives that was not to be repaired was stored outside the south end of the erecting shop, under a six-ton Goliath crane with a 75ft span. All tanks and tender tanks to be repaired went to a new tank shop built near the gantry crane.

Repairs were divided into four stages along the length of the erecting shop. Firstly stripping, examination and necessary cleaning; secondly frame and horn repairs, cylinder reboring and lining, and putting back the boiler; thirdly, refitting the wheels, tanks, rods, pistons, valves, injectors etc and fourthly, valve setting, refixing of piping and general finishing. For the last two stages, once the wheels had been replaced, the locomotives were drawn

through the shops by an electric winch fixed at the north end. Movement of parts about the shops was achieved through the use of four 50-ton cranes and two 6-ton overhead cranes. Smaller cranes were used in the adjoining machine shop, which had nearly 80 electrically driven machines arranged so that ones of the same general classification were grouped together.

The rearrangement of the older parts of the works is shown in another diagram. In the Lower Yard, the old repair shop was converted into a modern boiler shop equipped with two 25-ton overhead cranes and beyond this a new steaming shed was erected for mounting and testing boilers. The old machine shop was vacated, and the carpenters' shop, formerly above this, was brought down to ground level; one corner of this being set aside for an air-compressor and hydraulic power plant. Remaining from the former layout were the brass foundry, forge and smithy, the latter supplemented with a new spring-preparing furnace.

At the north end of the new erecting shop an engine weighbridge was installed, capable of weighing locomotives up to and including the 'King' class; plus a 70ft by 20ft examination house, equipped with a 1-ton overhead crane, and a scrapyard, served by a traverser. Installation of the weighbridge brought to an end the practice of

1933

A = Engine Weighbridge
B = Inspection Pit House
C = Shelter
D = Builders' Material
E = Boiler House
F = Offices
G = Brass Foundry
H = Carpenters
J = Tank Shop

S = Stores
T = Traverser
U = Coppersmiths
V = Pattern Store
W = Drawing Office
X = Toilets
Y = Timber

SCALE

0   100   500 FEET

83

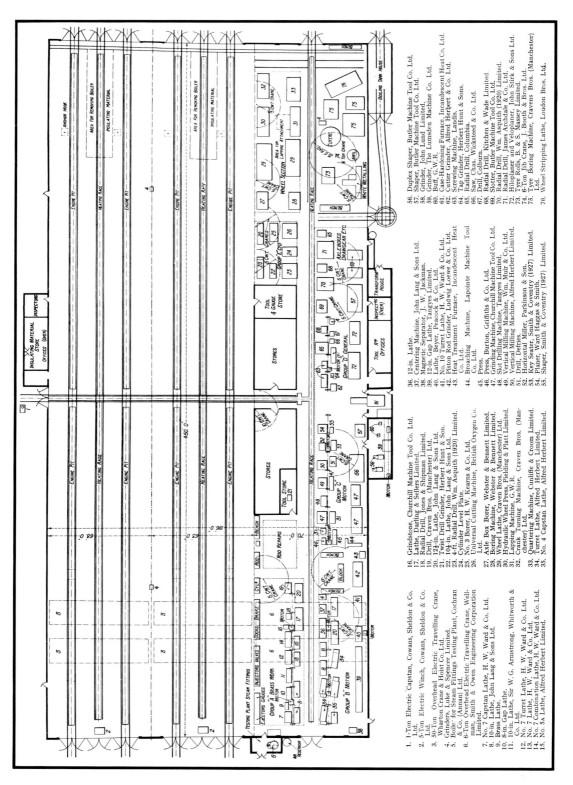

1. 1-Ton Electric Capstan, Cowans, Sheldon & Co. Ltd.
2. 5-Ton Electric Winch, Cowans, Sheldon & Co. Ltd.
3. 50-Ton Overhead Electric Travelling Crane, Wharton Crane & Hoist Co. Ltd.
4. Grinders, Luke & Spencer Limited.
5. Boiler for Steam Fittings Testing Plant, Cochran & Co. (Annan) Ltd.
6. 6-Ton Overhead Electric Travelling Crane, Wellman, Smith & Owen Engineering Corporation Limited.
7. No. 1 Capstan Lathe, H. W. Ward & Co. Ltd.
8. 10-in. Lathe, John Lang & Sons Ltd.
9. Brass Lathe.
10. 8-in. Gap Lathe.
11. 10-in. Lathe, Sir W. G. Armstrong, Whitworth & Co. Ltd.
12. No. 7 Turret Lathe, H. W. Ward & Co. Ltd.
13. No. 7 Lathe, H. W. Ward & Co. Ltd.
14. No. 7 Combination Lathe, H. W. Ward & Co. Ltd.
15. No. 4 Capstan Lathe, Alfred Herbert Limited.

16. Grindstone, Churchill Machine Tool Co. Ltd.
17. Lathe, Darling & Sellers Limited.
18. Radial Drill, Jones & Shipman Limited.
19. Drill, Craven Bros. (Manchester) Ltd.
20. 12½-in. Lathe, John Lang & Sons Ltd.
21. Twist Drill Grinder, Herbert Hunt & Son.
22. 10¼-in. Lathe, John Lang & Sons Ltd.
23. 4-ft. Radial Drill, Wm. Asquith (1920) Limited.
24. Cylinder Level Plate.
25. No. 3 Borer, H. W. Kearns & Co. Ltd.
26. Universal Cutting Machine, British Oxygen Co. Ltd.
27. Axle Box Borer, Webster & Bennett Limited.
28. Boring Machine, Webster & Bennett Limited.
29. Radial Drill, Craven Bros. (Manchester) Ltd.
30. Hydraulic Wheel Press, Fielding & Platt Limited.
31. Lapping Machine, G.W.R.
32. Crank Turning Machine, Craven Bros. (Manchester) Ltd.
33. Quartering Machine, Cunliffe & Croom Limited.
34. Turret Lathe, Alfred Herbert Limited.
35. Shaper, Smith & Coventry (1927) Limited.

36. 12-in. Lathe.
37. Centering Machine, John Lang & Sons Ltd.
38. Magnetic Separator, J. W. Jackman.
39. 12-in. Gap Lathe, Tangyes Limited.
40. Lathe, Beyer, Peacock & Co. Ltd.
41. No. 10 Turret Lathe, H. W. Ward & Co. Ltd.
42. Piston Rod Grinder, Ludwig Loewe & Co. Ltd.
43. Heat Treatment Furnace, Incandescent Heat Co. Ltd.
44. Broaching Machine, Lapointe Machine Tool Co. Ltd.
45. Press, Burton, Griffiths & Co. Ltd.
46. Press, Burton, Webster & Bennett Limited.
47. Grinding Machine, Churchill Machine Tool Co. Ltd.
48. Slot Drilling Machine, Wm. Muir & Co. Ltd.
49. Vertical Milling Machine, Wm. Muir & Co. Ltd.
50. Vertical Milling Machine, Alfred Herbert Limited.
51. Drill, Defries.
52. Horizontal Miller, Parkinson & Son.
53. Key Seater, Smith & Coventry (1927) Limited.
54. Planer, Ward Haggas & Smith.
55. Shaper, Smith & Coventry (1927) Limited.

56. Duplex Shaper, Butler Machine Tool Co. Ltd.
57. Shaper, Butler Machine Tool Co. Ltd.
58. Grinder, John Lund Limited.
59. Grinder, The Lumsden Machine Co. Ltd.
60. Buff, G.W.R.
61. Case-Hardening Furnace, Incandescent Heat Co. Ltd.
62. Cutter Grinder, Alfred Herbert & Co. Ltd.
63. Screwing Machine, Landis.
64. Tap Grinder, Herbert Hunt & Sons.
65. Radial Drill, Columbia.
66. Saw, Chas. Wicksteed & Co. Ltd.
67. Drill, Colburn.
68. Radial Drill, Kitchen & Wade Limited.
69. Slotter, Butler Machine Tool Co. Ltd.
70. Radial Drill, Wm. Asquith (1920) Limited.
71. Radial Drill, James Archdale & Co. Ltd.
72. Hiloplaner and Veloplaner, John Stirk & Sons Ltd.
73. Tyre Rolls, B. & S. Massey Limited.
74. 6-Ton Jib Crane, J. Booth & Bros. Ltd.
75. Tyre Boring Machine, Cravens Bros. (Manchester) Ltd.
76. Wheel Stripping Lathe, Loudon Bros. Ltd.

Above:

One of the casualties of the redevelopment of Stafford Road works was its crane engine No 17 *Cyclops*, nicknamed 'Cycleclips' by the workers there. Withdrawn in December 1933, after working there since November 1903, it was put into store at Swindon before being broken up there in 1938.
Bucknall Collection/Ian Allan Library

Left:

The locomotive erecting and machine shops as completed in 1932. *Railway Gazette*

Below:

The new Stafford Road works in full swing (sic) during the 1930s, with George Skidmore, he of the bowler hat, the shop foreman, overseeing the movement of 2-6-2T No 5136 over one of the new erecting shop's eight pits.
Ned Williams Collection

sending repaired locomotives to Tyseley (formerly the nearest weighbridge) to be weighed. This had also been their test run prior to painting and final finishing. Also ousted by the works modernisation was its crane engine, No 17 *Cyclops* which was transferred to the yard outside A shop at Swindon in December 1933.

Thus, in a little over three years, Stafford Road works had been changed from a cramped and rundown Victorian establishment into a modern locomotive repair depot, capable of receiving any class of locomotive then running on the GWR. Quite quickly, the examination house became known as 'The Clinic', and no amount of modernisation could remove the tag of 'The Museum' which the works had acquired due to the large numbers of older classes of locomotive, especially ex-Cambrian ones, which found their way there for repair.

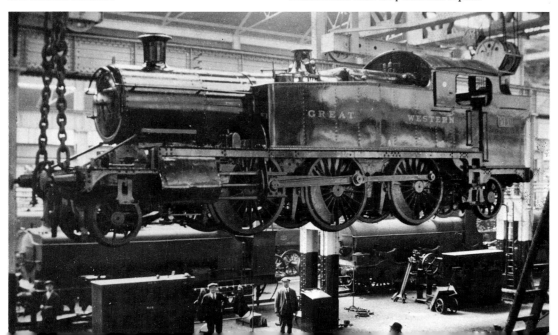

Above:
A study in concentration. Only the foreman (trilby hat this time), appears agitated as a locomotive is rewheeled. A photograph taken by the *Wolverhampton Chronicle* to illustrate an article on 21 March 1960 referring to the rundown of Stafford Road works.
Wolverhampton Chronicle/Ned Williams Collection

Interest often surrounds details of the capacity of locomotive works, and the length of time engines spent there. Appendix 4 presents monthly lists of all the locomotives noted in Stafford Road works during 1938, when its operation was at its height in the prewar period.

Nationalisation brought a few immediate changes. During the week ending 24 January 1948, ex-GWR 0-6-0 tender engine No 2323 (the second oldest such locomotive still running on Western Region) became the last to be lettered 'GWR' at Stafford Road, and 2-6-2T engine No 6126 was the first to be lettered 'BRITISH RAILWAYS', in hand-painted yellow letters, edged in red. Throughout the 1950s, Stafford Road continued to receive and maintain its familiar mixture of ex-GWR locomotives, plus the growing numbers of BR Standard classes that were introduced into the area.

The Rundown and Closure of Stafford Road Works

Evidence that steam locomotive repair facilities, such as those at Stafford Road, had only a short future was provided by British Railways Modernisation Plan, published in January 1955, which opted for diesel traction. It was therefore obvious to many that further changes would be likely at the works, and that these would entail redundancies. But few

Above:
**Despite its rundown, Stafford Road works still played
host to parties of local schoolchildren, such as this
group pictured amongst the 16XX, 84XX and 53XX bits
and pieces littering the erecting shop in 1961.**
Wolverhampton Chronicle/Ned Williams Collection

were prepared for the announcement that the whole
works would close, which was made by the British
Transport Commission (BTC) on 26 May 1959. This
began what must have been a most trying and
frustrating time for all those working at Stafford
Road.

Closure of the works meant the loss of 600 jobs,
and Wolverhampton Council passed a resolution of
alarm at this at its June 1959 meeting. Whether or
not this reached the ears of the BTC is not known,
but on 15 July 1959 it announced plans for siting a
diesel repair works at Stafford Road, to employ

about 100. The year 1960 brought further encourage-
ment. On 29 January the BTC announced that there
could be diesel work for upwards of 300 at Stafford
Road, and that, in any case, steam repair work
would continue longer than previously predicted.
Then, later in the year, on 3 September, the BTC
made the announcement that everyone wanted to
hear: 'Stafford Road locomotive works will not close.
It will maintain and repair diesels.' A further
announcement on 7 September noted the necessity of
making good certain shortages of skilled labour and
apprentices that had occurred at the works over
recent years.

Its future seemingly assured, Stafford Road works
weathered 1961 and the first half of 1962, although
the workforce dropped from 600 to 400. Then on
23 August 1962, the BTC announced a general
reduction of 20,000 in the workforce at its main
railway workshops over the next five years under a

Railway Workshops Reorganisation Plan; details would be announced later. These came on 19 September, when it was stated that Stafford Road would close in 1964, but that it might become a Western Region running maintenance shop. Local Trades Councils protested over the loss of the 360 shop floor and 40 clerical jobs; and protest strikes at the major BR workshops throughout that October persuaded the BTC to reprieve 3,000 jobs nationwide, but this did not save Stafford Road.

Notice of its final closure came on 21 August 1963, when the BTC rather coldly announced that Stafford Road works 'will cease to function on 1 June 1964', and that the payroll rundown would begin on 18 October 1963; 100 of the 200 remaining jobs to go by Christmas. With cruel irony, that October also saw the withdrawal of ex-GWR 2-6-2T No 4507, the last Wolverhampton-built locomotive still working on BR. A call by the Wolverhampton *Express & Star* newspaper to preserve this engine was met by the bald reply from BR that 'It is not on the list of locomotives to be preserved'.

On 11 February 1964 it fell to ex-GWR 2-8-0 locomotive No 2859 to have the dubious distinction of being the last engine to be overhauled at Stafford Road; photographs were taken of the event, and No 2859 set off en route to South Wales, leaving the works 130 employees with nothing to do.

Following closure a buyer for the 10½-acre works site was found quickly, it being sold 'subject to contract' on 12 November, two months after the last Wolverhampton-built locomotive still working, 0-6-0T No 2092, was cut up by the NCB at Bargoed.

Left:
Doomed but still working. 56XX and 84XX engines undergo repair at Stafford Road works in 1962.
Simon Dewey

Left:
The last Wolverhampton-built locomotive to run on BR — '45XX' class 2-6-2T No 4507 — is seen at Swindon on 20 December 1959. *Dr J. A. Coiley*

Above:
The end of 115 years of locomotive repairs came on 11 February 1964 when 2-8-0 No 2859 was outshopped at Stafford Road works. The gentleman second left seems to have got his expression about right.
J. Yates Collection, via F. G. Richardson

Right:
All that remained. The true monument to Stafford Road works, the first 10 steps that once led up to the GWR Mechanics Institute, photographed on 26 May 1988, and demolished shortly afterwards. *Author*

5: Wolverhampton's Railways from 1963 to the Present

The latter part of 1962 was a period of great reorganisation for Britain's railways. Under provisions of a new Transport Act (1962), which came into force on 1 September, the BTC was dissolved, and railway control was placed under a new British Railways Board (BRB). This delegated many managerial and operational functions to Regional Railway Boards. Following nationalisation, ex-LMS lines in the Wolverhampton area had been controlled by the London Midland Region (LMR), and ex-GWR lines by Western Region (WR). But, under inter-Regional boundary changes, also announced that September, the latter relinquished control of an area to the LMR stretching from near Bicester through Barnt Green to the Welsh coast, north of Aberystwyth. This included the line through Birmingham, Wolverhampton and Shrewsbury to Chester. Later, on 1 July 1963, the LMR's 'Western lines' were divided into four divisions, based at Euston, Birmingham, Stoke-on-Trent and Chester, and all responsible to a Western Line Manager based at Crewe.

Although nominally only administrative, this regional transfer was to have the most profound effect upon the railways serving Wolverhampton, as millions of pounds was spent modernising them.

Below:
One of a series of aerial photographs taken in 1964 to assist in planning the 25kV electrification of the Euston-Crewe main line, showing Wolverhampton's High and Low Level stations before work commenced.
BICC Ltd

Electrification and Resignalling

Paragraph 43 of the BTC's *Modernisation and Re-equipment of British Railways* report, published in January 1955, identified two major trunk routes for electrification, one of which was the LMR main line from Euston to Birmingham, Crewe, Liverpool and Manchester. Little more was heard of this scheme until March 1957, when Lord Rusholme, Chairman of the London Midland Area Board, announced further modernisation plans whilst on a visit to Birmingham. Beginning that month, he said, a team of railway experts would reconnoitre stations, depots and lines on the Birmingham-Crewe line to enable detailed plans to be drawn up for its electrification. Their findings were incorporated into the BTC's revised Modernisation Plan, published on 23 July 1957, which accorded priority to electrification of the Euston-Birmingham-Wolverhampton-Liverpool-Manchester line, using a 25kV overhead collection system which had been pioneered by French railways. This was supported by the LMR's announcement on 13 December of a £5.5 million electrification scheme for West Midlands lines using the same system.

Work on the trunk route electrification began immediately at its northern end, the first 9½ miles, between Wilmslow and Mauldeth Road stations, opening on 26 November 1959; the first train being hauled by No E1000, a converted ex-GWR gas turbine locomotive. The whole scheme was divided into 44 stages covering 412 route-miles and over 1,500 miles of track, and was to be spread over 10

Above:
The progress of the electrification work north of the High Level station at Wolverhampton is shown in this view of Stanier Class 5 No 44776 on 17 May 1964 passing the works of the Electric Construction Co Ltd at Bushbury, and Wolverhampton No 1 box.
Michael Mensing

years. In addition to the laying in of 12 power feeder stations, 58 track section cabins and 109 relay rooms, it required clearance work under 649 bridges and through 27 tunnels, also encompassing the remodelling or reconstruction of 89 stations. Stages 1 to 21 focused upon the line south from Crewe to Euston via the Trent Valley line and both routes between Rugby and Wolverton, via Northampton and Blisworth. Work progressed so well that its scheduling was revised in February 1964, bringing the completion date forward to March 1967.

From Wolverhampton the electrification scheme included both the Grand Junction and Stour Valley lines to Birmingham, plus the line to Walsall and the ex-LNWR Soho loop line; thus preserving the operating flexibility enjoyed under steam with regard to the choice of route available and to the approach made to New Street station. Until electrified passenger services began on 6 March 1967, electric trains only used these lines for clearance tests or for freight workings.

Stage No	Section of line	Energised	First used
22	South of Stafford-North of High Level Station; Bushbury-Wednesfield Heath	Jan 1966	Mar 1966
23	Monmore Green-North of High Level station; Crane Street Junction-South of Portobello Junction	Sept 1966	Dec 1966
24(1)	Wednesfield Heath-Bescot	Jan 1966	Mar 1966
24(2)	Bescot-South of Aston; Perry Barr North and South Junctions-Handsworth Wood; Aston-Duddeston	July 1966	Oct 1966
24(3)	South of Portobello Junction-Walsall	Apr 1966	June 1966
25	Oldbury-Monmore Green	Oct 1966	Dec 1966
26	Monument Lane-Oldbury; Soho North and South Junctions-Soho	Oct 1966	Dec 1966
27	Monument Lane-Adderley Park and Duddeston	Oct 1966	Dec 1966
28	South of Aston and Adderley Park-South of Stechford	July 1966	Oct 1966
36	Soho-Handsworth Wood	Oct 1966	Dec 1966

This electrification scheme made increased speeds and service frequencies possible, but also required modernisation of the lines' signalling. The dozens of older signalboxes were unevenly spaced because their siting had originally depended on the position of stations, junctions and level crossings, and this had an irregular effect upon line capacity. Therefore, in tandem with electrification, the manually-worked semaphore signalling, with the exception of that around Stockport, was replaced with high beam-intensity colour-light signals, backed up by the Automatic Warning System of train control, a development from the GWR's Automatic Train Control.

Instead of the many signalboxes formerly controlling main line train movements, between Stafford and Coventry three large power boxes were built at Birmingham New Street, Walsall and Wolverhampton. Resignalling work began during 1963, the engineers involved taking the former offices of the Wolverhampton District Goods Manager as their base, occupying these until moving on to a northern signalling modernisation scheme early in 1971. Wolverhampton's power signalbox was sited at the south end of the High Level station, partly on the site of an old ARP shelter, and against the retaining wall overlooking the Low Level station. It was completed early in July 1965, and commissioned on 18 August that year. This controlled 23 route-miles, from a boundary with Stafford box at Littleton colliery, just north of the site of Four Ashes station, to a boundary with New Street box at Tipton station on the Stour Valley line, and to a boundary with Walsall box at Willenhall station on the Grand Junction line.

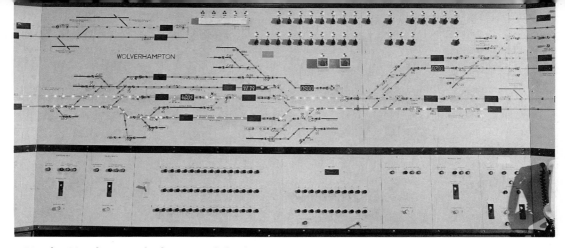

Above:
The control panel in Wolverhampton power box on its commissioning day, 18 August 1965. From here, 23 route miles were controlled, reaching from near Penkridge to Tipton and Willenhall.
British Railways, London Midland Region

March 1967 also saw the last use of the former GWR sidings at Oxley as a marshalling yard, although they continued to be used as freight sidings until March 1969. Their complete closure was prevented through use as carriage sidings for stock off the new electrified InterCity trains. When these began, most of the trains serving Wolverhampton were working through to or from Manchester or Liverpool, and only three daily Euston services began and terminated there. Consequently, their stock needed little siding space, and the need to change to a diesel locomotive to move this in and out of the High Level station caused only slight inconvenience. But, with the introduction of a half-hourly InterCity London service from May 1972, much of this would be reversed.

In preparation for this it was therefore decided to remodel the down side of Oxley sidings, the old Crewe and Birkenhead yards, plus the access roads to the former GWR locomotive depot, as carriage sidings; and to extend the overhead system across Oxley Viaduct into these, to enable electric locomotives to bring their own stock down from the High Level station. The gantries for this were erected in the autumn of 1971 and the overhead was first energised on 1 April 1972, this being the only ex-GWR line in the country to be electrified. Operation of these sidings proved successful and so various improvements were implemented. A £150,000 carriage washer was brought into use on 8 October 1974 with the capacity to clean 700 carriages per week, each 10-coach set using 23gal of acid and neutraliser, plus 700gal of water in the four-stage washing process. Situated beyond the limit of the overhead, moving stock through this required the use of a dual-braked Class 08 shunter. Additional capacity was created by the reinstatement of five sidings in the former up yard at Oxley in October 1976, and on 29 November an £800,000 Carriage Maintenance Depot was opened in the down yard, its 910ft two-road shed, capable of taking a 12-coach set, being erected on part of the site of the GWR's former locomotive depot. This can

undertake heavy repairs to carriages, including any requiring the removal of their bogies. Finally, in May 1985, the overhead wires at Oxley were extended a further 554yd, down as far as the carriage washer.

The Reconstruction of Wolverhampton High Level Station

One of the 89 stations mentioned earlier as being remodelled or reconstructed under the LMR's electrification scheme was Wolverhampton High Level, which was to be modernised and developed to replace both the old High and Low Level stations.

Much criticised, almost from its opening, by the late 1950s Wolverhampton High Level's facilities, last improved in the mid-1880s, were showing signs of neglect. It was, for example, still gas-lit. Given too its suffix, the station was an easy target for headlines in the local *Express & Star* of the 'Low Opinions at High Level' kind. Described by one regular passenger as 'a cross between a barracks and a wind tunnel', it boasted a rather slender and wan collection of amenities; two newspaper stalls (one closed most of the time), one buffet, and two waiting rooms. The latter serving Platforms 2 and 3 was described thus by a reporter one wet and chilly November morning:

'This 12ft by 8ft room contains one long wooden bench and one bench seat in green American cloth, ripped to pieces, and four prints darkly surly from age. There are also two doors, facing each other. If both happen to be used at the same time, one senses what Scott must have suffered at the Antarctic. Four passengers sat in shivering. A railway official came in and started putting coal in

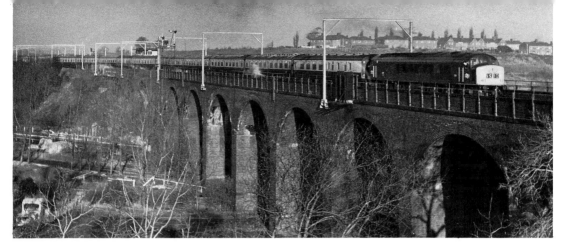

Above:
The electrification of Oxley carriage sidings. Class 45 No 134 brings a train of empty stock from the sidings across Oxley Viaduct to provide the 11.35 Birmingham New Street-Edinburgh via Derby relief service on 28 December 1971. *G. F. Bannister*

Below:
One of High Level's gas lights blazes away in broad daylight, emphasising the urgent need for rebuilding the station that existed when this view was taken around 1960. *D. Smith*

the cold stove. "We're getting organised, we're getting there," he said. He patted his pockets for some moments and then asked me: "Got a match?" '

Despite the services of men born ahead of their time, High Level station was clearly in need of improvement; and so the announcement, on 27 February 1959, that it was to be reconstructed under a £500,000 scheme was generally welcomed. The diversion of most London services to the Low Level station from that 2 November seemed to indicate that work would start soon; but it did not, and these trains were not restored for eight years, rather than in the four years expected. Surprisingly, further details of the scheme were not announced until January 1962, when it was said to involve 'the remodelling of the track lay-out, station buildings and lengthening of platforms . . . . The completed scheme will effect a great improvement in accommodation and facilities, a changeover from gas to electricity, a new subway and lifts for parcels traffic and [the replacement of] four manually operated [signalboxes].'

The new Wolverhampton High Level was designed by R. L. Moorcroft, Architect to the LMR, his preliminary plans being prepared by 19 October 1961. Under these, the old station's main buildings were to be retained and remodelled internally,

whilst its overall roof was to be removed. A second island platform was to be added, with this and the existing island platform having new waiting and refreshment rooms built on them. However, examination of the old buildings showed structural weaknesses, which, together with other alterations, required the revision of the remodelling scheme and the adoption of a more radical reconstruction; the finalised plans for which were approved on 30 October 1963. Only the original platforms were now to be retained and extended; new station buildings would be erected.

Reconstruction work began finally on 19 February 1964, and was divided into three phases. Phase 1 involved track remodelling, beginning with the lines serving Platform 3, plus platform extensions, mainly at the Birmingham end, beginning with island Platform 2 and 3. This would allow longer trains to

be accommodated and permit Platforms 1 and 2 to be used by trains entering the station from both directions. Once the platforms were extended, a temporary wooden footbridge was erected across the extensions to permit the removal of the old footbridge.

Below:
D295 arrives at Wolverhampton High Level with the 12.25 Birmingham New Street-Glasgow service on 28 August 1964. The temporary footbridge had been erected for use whilst the station was being rebuilt. *A. J. Wheeler*

Bottom:
With the roof removed on 22 February 1965, Wolverhampton High Level reveals details of its 1884 reconstruction previously hidden from view. The photographer is standing on the temporary footbridge shown in the last photograph. *L. J. Lee*

Above:
The exterior of the new Wolverhampton High Level station nears completion in this March 1967 view from the forecourt. *Mrs P. Norton*

Right:
April 1967, and the brave new railway comes to Wolverhampton. According to complaints received about the new 'moan' station when it opened, our friend with the briefcase would need more than his mac if the weather turned nasty! *Brian Haresnape*

Phase 2 included the demolition of the existing buildings and began on 25 January 1965 with the awarding of a £100,000 contract to Tarmac Ltd. This phase also marked the only day on which the station had to be closed, 22 February 1965, when the overall roof was brought down by cutting it into sections and dropping them on to the tracks and platforms. Demolition of the remaining sections of the station began in mid-October 1965, with the façade toppling to the street on 11 January 1966. Shortly thereafter, Phase 3, including the new building, could begin.

As part of this, the junction between the High Level and ex-S&B lines, removed in October 1859, was reinstated to allow the diversion of trains from Shrewsbury and Wellington away from the Low Level station into the High Level; the reinstatement being completed on 6 August 1966. All work, except that on the forecourt, was finished in time for the inauguration of the electrified service on 6 March 1967.

The new High Level was an instant . . . failure! Within two months of its opening the *Express & Star* was back with: 'New Rail era means low spirits at High Level', echoing public complaints about the shortness of the platform canopies, the cramped buffet, and the total lack of any facilities on the island platform. These remarks did not go unheeded, and on 27 July 1967 the *Express & Star* was able to report BR's 'New Plan for "Moan" Station', which included two additional waiting rooms, extra toilet facilities, and a refreshment room on the island platform, plus 120ft of additional platform canopies; to be completed by the end of the year. Some criticisms still remained, particularly concerning the buffet, and a further round of improvements were planned in December 1970; work beginning on 3 September 1971 on a £15,000 scheme to enlarge the booking and inquiry office space at the same time.

More recent years have seen continuing improvements at Wolverhampton station, which officially lost its 'High Level' suffix in 1973. The old north bay siding, serving a former goods storage shed, was remodelled into a curving bay platform, which was numbered 1c and electrified in time for the start of the 1979-80 timetable on 15 May 1979; although it is mainly used by the DMU, latterly Sprinter, local services to Shrewsbury. Car parking had long been a problem at the station. Some use had been made of adjacent land set aside for the completion of Wolverhampton's ring road (and later an unopened portion of this), but as this was only temporary a more permanent solution was sought. A multi-storey car park was therefore planned by the station from February 1983, and opened in 1985.

All of this investment finally paid off when, on 22 March 1984, Wolverhampton was named as Station of the Year — 1983; having beaten 13 other LMR main line stations to the title. It also took part in Wolverhampton's Millennium Celebrations in 1985, when on 21 June that year locomotive No 86433 was named *Wulfruna* there by the town's Mayor, Councillor George Howells. Just behind *Wulfruna* on Platform 3 that day was the GWR 150 Exhibition Train; its presence *there* providing a timely reminder of the other story of Wolverhampton's railways since 1963.

The Rundown of the 'Great Western' in Wolverhampton

In contrast to the above, the former GWR lines ceded to the LMR on 1 January 1963 saw none of the millions that were spent modernising the railways

Above:

A stranger at High Level. 'Westerns' were once a common sight at Low Level, but the appearance of D1037 *Western Empress* at the High Level on 24 January 1975, working the 10.59 to Paddington via Coventry, was a rarity brought about by the Bushey derailment the previous day. *M. C. Barker*

Below:

Another stranger at High Level. No 33012 brings a Portsmouth-Wolverhampton relief into the High Level on 12 August 1978. Having worked the stock throughout, it returned with its ecs shortly afterwards. *A. Swift*

serving Wolverhampton. Indeed, they were already depleted through the withdrawal of local passenger services to Stourbridge along the ex-OWW main line five months earlier, although the line at least remained open for seven up and eight down trains per day; mostly parcels services to Stourbridge or

Hartlebury, plus one through Crewe-Bristol parcels train and one pigeon train to Great Malvern, plus their return workings. It also saw regular use by through Sunday passenger services, notably the 1.40pm Crewe-Plymouth service, from November 1963, and the 11am Liverpool-Plymouth and the 2.45pm Plymouth-Liverpool trains, which were re-routed via Wellington, Wolverhampton, Stourbridge and Worcester Shrub Hill from 1 November 1964.

These services continued until March 1967, from when the line saw only freight workings and diversions occasioned by clearance restrictions under the West Coast main line's 25kV overhead wires, such as on Sunday 9 April 1967 when newly restored ex-LNER 'A4' Pacific No 60010 *Dominion of Canada* was hauled over it en route from Crewe to London's Victoria Docks for shipment to Canada, a gift from the BRB to the Canadian Railroad Historical Association's museum in Montreal.

From 1963 a curious operating system now existed on Wolverhampton's 'Great Western' lines, under which all former WR local services were run by the LMR, but the Paddington to Birkenhead and West Coast through services etc, now strictly speaking inter-Regional ones, continued to be operated by the WR. Change was also apparent, most noticeably in the continuing programme of conversion to diesel traction, removing the need for two steam sheds; and so Stafford Road, being in the worst state of repair, closed on 9 September 1963, its allocation being transferred to Oxley which was renumbered 2B on the same day (Bushbury becoming 2K).

With the degree of investment being ploughed into the Euston-Northwest electrification, the future of the Wolverhampton-Paddington alternative route must have long seemed in doubt; although the lack of any reference to its closure in *The Reshaping of British Railways* or Beeching Report may have given cause for optimism. Not for long though. On 21 April 1964 the LMR announced that Wolverhampton Low Level station would close in 1967, and the Beeching Report had actually said that the future of such parallel routes was 'being determined'. The fruit of these deliberations appeared in a second report: *The Development of the Major Trunk Routes*, published in February 1965, which did not pull its punches. All competing routes were compared on five criteria: *General* (areas linked and the projected traffic flows between these), *Physical* (the number of bridges, tunnels, ruling gradients and speed restrictions, etc), *Traffic levels* (at present), *Alternative routes* (salient features of), and *'Network' considerations* (how the route fitted in with future needs). On these criteria, the Euston route won out hands down; and whilst this only meant that the ex-GWR route would not enjoy development, it was clear that this actually meant that it would suffer closure.

Meanwhile, other links with the 'GWR' at Wolverhampton were being severed. The B&W Wombourn line was officially closed on 1 March 1965. Tettenhall and Wombourn stations had closed to freight on 6 July 1964, and the last scheduled train, a freight working from Evesham to Crewe, ran on 27 February 1965. Of course this was not really the last train to use the line. On 2 March a weedkilling train passed over it, and the distinction of being the *very* last train to use the line fell to a diverted out-of-gauge freight running on 24 June 1965. The line remained *in situ* throughout 1966; but following closure of Oxley North, the signalbox controlling its junction with the ex-S&B line, track lifting began on 30 May 1967 back as far as Pensnett, and was completed by January 1968, by which time the line had all but reverted to the ex-OWW Kingswinford branch it had begun as in 1913.

The rundown of the 'Great Western' in Wolverhampton was also most noticeable in changes to the train service. These generally took the form of service reductions, such as the curtailment of the daily working to Sussex and the Kent Coast to run on Saturdays only from 8 September 1963, and the short working of the 13.10, 17.10 and 19.10 Paddington-Birkenhead services only as far as Wolverhampton, from 20 June 1964, with the three corresponding up services starting from there, and other services north of Wolverhampton being operated by connecting DMUs. There were slight service improvements, such as the re-routeing and acceleration of the 'Pines Express' from 8 September 1963, and the restoration of 1hr 55min Snow Hill-Paddington timings on the 'Birmingham Pullman' from 26 June 1964; but the general trend in services was towards their rundown. Even heightened periods of activity, occasioned by the periodic diversion of Sunday services away from Birmingham New Street in April, May and September 1965, to hasten its reconstruction, did little to allay this impression.

There were noticeable motive power changes too, not all of which centred around the withdrawal of steam. The initial teething troubles experienced with the 'Western' diesel-hydraulics from their introduction on the Paddington trains persisted, and after a year their replacement with the new diesel-electric Brush Type 4s (now Class 47s) was announced. The first of these locomotives arrived at Tyseley for crew training on 18 November 1963, and they were scheduled to assume the Western's duties from 16 December, but this was deferred until 23 December as the training programme was not complete, and then cancelled when it was discovered that they were fitted with standard BR AWS equipment which was incompatible with the Great Western ATC-derived AWS equipment fitted to the former WR lines in the West Midlands. So it was not until 14 January 1964 that D1682-7, D1695-6 and D1699 (Nos 47096, 47485, 47097-47100, 47107-8 and 47111) finally took up their duties between Padding-

Above:
'Castle' class No 7001 *Sir James Milne* **leaves Wolverhampton Low Level with the southbound 'Pines Express', passing No 6930** *Aldersey Hall* **on a northbound freight, which has just come off the ex-OWW line, closed to passengers from 30 July 1962.** *Ian Allan Library*

Right:
An LMR express, now worked by the WR, at a LMR station, that once belonged to the GWR! As if to highlight the curious circumstances under which Wolverhampton Low Level operated after 1 January 1963, Castle Class No 7001 *Sir James Milne* **awaits departure with the southbound 'Pines Express'. A view taken a few minutes before the previous photograph, on 7 May 1963.** *Ian Allan Library*

ton and Shrewsbury. The 'Pines Express' remained the only regular 'Western' duty in the West Midlands in the spring of 1964 until it too was turned over to the Brush Type 4s in mid-March that year. Hydraulic traction was not lost to the area though as by the November and December of 1964 the Brush locomotives were proving about as reliable as the 'Westerns' they had replaced, and a series of failures hastened the latter's return, together with a number of 'Hymeks', in contravention of a LMR ban on the use of hydraulic traction, while the problems with the Brush Type 4s were ironed out. These substitutions lasted until April 1965.

By this time steam locomotives were still being used extensively on the former WR lines in the Wolverhampton area, working the vast majority of freight services and most of the passenger services north from the town and services to the west as far as Bristol and south as far as Banbury. The end of May 1964 had even seen the return of a number of 'Castle' class locomotives to Oxley shed to work the Shrewsbury and Birkenhead trains northwards. The end of steam working into and out of Western Region was officially marked on 27 November 1965. Brush Type 4s were introduced on freight workings on the LMR lines in the West Midlands, including the ex-WR ones, on 3 January 1966, but the use of steam persisted, especially on summer Saturday extra services, notably to Pwllheli, which were rostered for steam haulage, mainly by BR Standard Class 4 locomotives. But following the end of the

1966 summer timetable the pace of steam withdrawal accelerated noticeably until eventually steam passenger working was confined to the Wolverhampton-Shrewsbury leg of the 15.10 Paddington to Shrewsbury service on Mondays to Fridays. This was the sole remaining mile-a-minute steam passenger working on British Railways; the locomotives concerned returning to Wolverhampton with the 21.36 Shrewsbury-Paddington parcels train.

Four days — 3-6 March 1967 — witnessed the virtual elimination of the 'GWR' from Wolverhampton. On Friday 3 March Oxley shed closed, its remaining allocation being 20 Class 5 and Class 8

goods locomotives, but like most other official closures this was not quite the end of its story as steam locomotives continued to be sent there from Crewe for wheel turning and other maintenance until the final elimination of steam from BR in August 1968. Oxley sidings also ceased to be used as a marshalling yard, but also survived their later official closure date of 3 October 1967 through the continued running of a steam-hauled freight service between Oxley and Crewe (Gresty Lane). The last

'Birmingham Pullman' also ran on Friday 3 March, the sets being moved to London over that weekend to inaugurate a new 'South Wales Pullman' service between Paddington and Swansea from Monday 6 March.

Saturday and Sunday 4 and 5 March 1967 saw the running of 'Last Steam Specials' over the Paddington-Birkenhead line which closed with effect from Monday 6 March as the electrified Manchester-Liverpool-Wolverhampton High Level-Euston service commenced. Local services between Low Level station, Birmingham Snow Hill and stations beyond to Leamington Spa continued, but the majority of local trains serving Wellington and Shrewsbury were diverted to the High Level station.

Freight services along the ex-OWW line were the next to go, with the closure of the line between Priestfield and Dudley on 1 January 1968; this being taken out of use on 22 September 1968, and taken up shortly afterwards. A short single line section of this was retained just north of the site of Dudley station, as far as the bridge over the Birmingham New Road, to serve as a headshunt for the newly installed Dudley Freightliner terminal which had opened on 16 July 1967.

The last scheduled trains to use the tunnel at the south end of Birmingham Snow Hill did so on 2 March 1968; and the 17.15 service from Wellington became the last to call at Dunstall Park, the four remaining Shrewsbury-Low Level trains being diverted to Wolverhampton High Level from 4 March. The same day a shuttle service between the Low Level and Snow Hill was inaugurated. This was

Left:
The 'Birkenhead Flyer' pauses at Wolverhampton Low Level behind No 4079 *Pendennis Castle* on 4 March 1967, one of the last steam specials organised to coincide with the closure of the Paddington-Birkenhead through route. This one was organised by Ian Allan Ltd.
Mike Wood

Below left:
A rather grimy No 6862 *Derwent Grange* brings a goods train off the ex-OWW main line towards Wolverhampton Low Level in the mid-1960s. The Midland Railway-built link to the station can be seen on the left. The OWW line closed completely between Priestfield and Dudley on 1 January 1968. *Simon Dewey*

Below:
The Low Level-Snow Hill shuttle. A Gloucester-built single unit has arrived at Wolverhampton with the 17.48 from Birmingham in June 1969; one month after the introduction of conductor/guard operation on the line had allowed all of its stations to be de-staffed.
N. D. Griffiths

operated initially by three-car DMU sets, but poor passenger loadings saw the substitution of Class 122 single-car units from 5 August 1968, and the introduction of conductor/guards from 5 May 1969, allowing *all* of the stations it served to become unstaffed from that day.

The track north of Low Level station had remained *in situ*, seeing occasional use by freight trains, one passing over this at 00.43 on 27 July 1969 being the last to do so. In addition, at weekends between 6 November 1965 and 7 August 1966, the 'Bushbury Spur' Cannock Road Junction-Bushbury line had been used by northbound services diverted away from the High Level station by engineering work to reinstate the connection with the ex-S&B line at Wolverhampton North Junction. This was first used on 22 August by a freight train, the first passenger working over it being a Derby-Aberystwyth excursion on 17 September 1966.

Following the end of through working via Low Level station, track was lifted between the latter and just below the bridge carrying the Cannock Road over the railway. A spur was left to allow merry-go-round (MGR) hopper trains, carrying coal from the Cannock Chase and South Staffordshire coalfields to Ironbridge power station, to reverse and gain access to the ex-S&B line via the Cannock

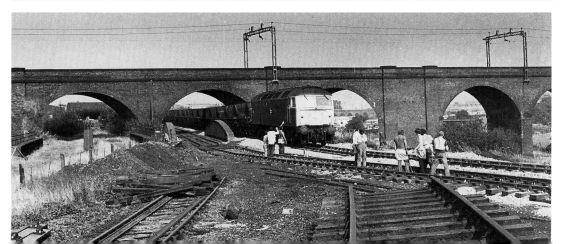

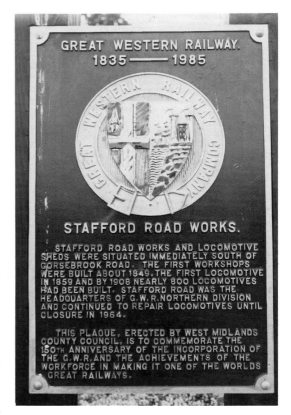

Road Junction-Stafford Road Junction line; these alterations coming into use from 18 January 1970.

Unfortunately, the 1 in 75 gradient under the Cannock Road bridge restricted the maximum load of trains performing this reversal to 800 tons, any train heavier than this having to reverse in the High Level station. On 8 November 1982, a £721,000 scheme was announced to construct a chord line, linking the Bushbury and Stafford Road Junction lines, eliminating both Cannock Road Junction and the need for all such reversals. The Oxley Chord consists of 320yd of double track, and was built to so tight a curvature that it has to carry check rails along its entire length. It was opened on 9 August 1983 and, with the removal of the remains of Cannock Road Junction, released 50 acres of land for sale.

The Low Level-Snow Hill shuttle service continued throughout 1969 and 1970, during which time the regular passengers and train crews established a very friendly relationship. And so when, on 31 March 1971, British Rail announced the line was for closure on 4 October, claiming the saving of £90,000 per annum, plus £22,000 in signalling costs, the passengers organised a protest in the form of a leaflet campaign. Their stance was supported by Wolverhampton Council, but to no avail. Closure was only deferred until 4 March 1972, when the departure of the 17.47 to Snow Hill (a three-car DMU put on to cope with expected numbers that did not materialise) also marked the final closure of Low Level station.

In almost exactly five years, the 'GWR' had been erased from Wolverhampton: Little remained. The line formerly used by the Snow Hill shuttle service was taken out of use as far as Stow Heath, adjacent to Wolverhampton Steel Terminal, on 23 May 1973, and lifted; the remaining double-track portion between there and Wednesbury being designated the 'Up Goods Departure' and 'Down Goods Arrival' lines on 7 December 1973. Ironically, Low Level's remaining rail connection, to Heath Town Junction,

had been built by the Midland Railway. Now this served to give access to the Parcels Concentration Depot that the station was converted into, until these lines were also taken out of use in October 1984; but at the time of writing they remain in place.

To coincide with the Wolverhampton Millennium and GWR 150 celebrations, the town council decided to build a memorial to its GWR associations. A site was chosen on the Stafford Road, near to the former Locomotive Works, the £16,500 'commemorative area' being opened on 21 November 1985. Sadly, the Council's £9,000 offer for a more solid reminder of the GWR, in the form of locomotive No 2859, the last to be overhauled at Stafford Road works and one of the last to remain at Barry, was unsuccessful; No 2859 arriving at the Llangollen Railway on 2 November 1987.

The Fall and Rise of Wolverhampton Low Level Station

Its fate sealed from 21 April 1964, Low Level station assumed an air of quiet resignation, which the bustle of the augmented service to Paddington could do nothing to dispel. As the end approached, little things assumed a disproportionate importance, and the announcement, on 2 February 1967, that the refreshment room drinks licence would not be

Above:
Comment is superfluous! *Ian R. Smith*

Below:
Wolverhampton Low Level after conversion to a Parcels Concentration Depot in April 1970. The photographer is standing on the site of the former South signalbox, closed on 23 May 1973, and the 'bridge', constructed to connect the raised platforms, is just visible behind the stop blocks. *M. C. Doubleday*

renewed when it expired shortly, received press coverage! Successive blows, from closure as a main line station through to destaffing, wrought few major changes in its appearance, until track lifting began at the north end in January 1970.

This was part of a £30,000 scheme to convert the station into a Parcels Concentration Depot (PCD), under which the four roads through the platforms were stopped off; three being truncated two-thirds of the way towards the north end the one alongside the up platform being stopped *at* the north end. All other trackwork was removed, the bay platforms were filled in, the North signalbox was closed and demolished, a platform-level solid concrete 'bridge' was built across the ends of the three shorter roads, and 10in of concrete was added to the platform surfaces; both of the latter being to allow BRUTE platform trolleys to be loaded and unloaded from either side without the use of ramps.

Wolverhampton PCD opened on 6 April 1970 and was fully commissioned that 4 May, claiming a capacity to handle 8,000 parcels daily and boasting a fleet of nearly 50 road vehicles. The end of the Snow Hill shuttle passenger service in March 1972 gave the PCD greater capacity, and by July 1976, the depot's *Guide to Parcels Delivery Rounds* ran to 267 pages, listing the streets included on its 57 rounds, which reached from Cannock to Kidderminster. Yet, under four years later, changes in British Rail's policy towards ending the collection of parcels (implemented, but more recently reversed) brought rumours of the PCD's closure, which were denied by the Chairman, Sir Peter Parker. Nevertheless close it did, officially from 1 June 1981; the last regular railborne parcels movement out of the depot departing on 12 June.

Two closures inside 10 years nurtured local fears regarding the future of the station buildings. But, from the 1950s, the station had also accommodated staff of the British Railways Divisional Engineer's Department, who remained in occupation following its closure as a PCD. Then, unexpectedly, as a result

of a conversation between local Council officials and British Rail management at the *Wulfruna* naming ceremony on 21 June 1985, a scheme was developed for the Council to buy the station and develop it as a transport museum. Independently, moves had been started in 1984, from within the then West Midlands County Council, to get the Low Level buildings listed; which they were, as Grade II, on 25 March 1986.

Above:
The buildings at Wolverhampton Low Level were listed as Grade II on 25 March 1986, following an initiative started by the outgoing West Midlands County Council. *Author*

Below:
The booking hall at Wolverhampton Low Level after demolition of the partition built in 1923; revealing a view unseen for 64 years. *David Peters Photography*

Left:
The excavated Wellington bay at Low Level, where short stubs of mixed gauge rail were found in 1986.
Author

Below left:
Short stubs of mixed gauge rail found at Wolverhampton Low Level station during excavation of the Wellington bay platform on 22 July 1986. *Author*

of the MSC and the station's fate is once more in the hands of local politicians and vandals. Whatever happens, the restoration work has already uncovered some curious finds. Perhaps the best known of these was made on 22 July 1986, when three stubs of mixed gauge track were found embedded in the end of the old Wellington bay platform. One suspects that Wolverhampton's 'station that refuses to die' has a few more surprises in store.

The Development of Passenger and Freight Services Since 1963

The face of Wolverhampton's railways has been completely altered by the combined effect of electrification and the rundown of the former GWR lines. The changes brought about in the last quarter of a century are reflected in the way both passenger services, local and InterCity, and freight services and facilities have been developed.

1 — Local passenger services

Electrification changed the pattern of local services from the High Level station. One casualty was the DMU-operated service to Burton-on-Trent, which was announced for withdrawal on 29 October 1963. Despite a newspaper campaign to save it, launched in April 1964, the last train ran on 16 January 1965; Willenhall (Bilston Street), Darlaston, and all of the intermediate stations to Alrewas, closing on the same day.

To maintain the high speeds along the electrified Stour Valley line required by both main line expresses and local EMU-operated services, some of the intermediate stations were closed and removed. Ettingshall Road & Bilston closed to passengers on 15 June 1964, and the freight-only Albion station closed that 10 August; freight services also being withdrawn from Monmore Green on 4 October 1965. The same day, Wednesfield, Wednesfield Heath and Bushbury stations, long closed to passengers, closed to freight as well.

From 6 March 1967 Wolverhampton High Level's local services consisted of an hourly EMU-operated Stour Valley line service to Birmingham New Street, which called at all stations and departed at 15min past the hour; and a DMU-operated all-stations service to Shrewsbury, every other train also working through to Chester. Penkridge, the sole

Wolverhampton Council bought the Low Level station in May 1986, the remaining British Rail staff leaving on 2 May. Six days later, a Wolverhampton Task Force, part of the Community Programme sponsored by the MSC, moved in to begin work on a four-stage programme of repair and renovation. Stage 1 involved clearing accumulated rubbish, excavating the former bay platforms, and emergency remedial work to the chimneys and pediment, plus reroofing and damp-proofing work undertaken by outside contractors. Stage 2 included demolition of the partition built by the GWR in the booking office and the removal of the concrete 'bridge' and the 10in-thick platform covering installed in 1970. Stage 3 will encompass reconstruction of the booking hall, and Stage 4, conversion of the buildings on the up platform into a caretaker's flat.

The future use of the Low Level station has yet to be decided, although early thoughts of developing some form of transport museum there have been discounted for the present. It may be used as some form of heritage centre, telling 'The Wolverhampton Story', of which, as we have seen, transport is a major component. Unfortunately, co-ordinated restoration work ceased at the Low Level with the end

Above:
An aerial view of the two Wolverhampton stations taken in the late 1970s. This affords an interesting comparison with the aerial photograph reproduced at the beginning of this chapter. Sadly, the large white-roofed building being put up to the rear of the Low Level is not a modern extension to it, just another DIY superstore. *Wolverhampton Library*

remaining intermediate station on the line to Stafford, was served by EMU-operated Manchester stopping trains.

On paper at least, the new Wolverhampton-Shrewsbury-Chester DMUs provided a considerably more ample service than the former Paddington-Birkenhead service which it in part replaced, especially to Shrewsbury. Discounting the disadvantage of a change of trains at Wolverhampton, Shrewsbury was now only just over 3hr from London, albeit Euston, compared to 3½hr by the axed 'GWR' route; and the service was hourly. Unfortunately, the 13 Gloucester cross-country and Metro-Cammell three-car DMU sets allocated to Chester depot to operate this service suffered a series of failures: five having been withdrawn, some through fires, by 22 April, and their two-car replacements were also plagued by the overcrowding and poor timekeeping that typified this service in its early months.

A much more minor change on the ex-S&B line concerned the name of Birches & Bilbrook Halt.

Together with many of the other ex-GWR halts in the country this officially lost its 'Halt' suffix in the late 1960s, becoming Birches & Bilbrook with effect from 6 May 1968, and the even plainer Bilbrook from 6 May 1974.

Local services came under the control of the West Midlands Passenger Transport Executive (WMPTE), under an agreement signed with British Rail on 12 January 1973, which was backdated to 1 January 1972. Under this the WMPTE paid British Rail a grant calculated on the same basis as the Government's current grant to BR for these services. In practice, the Government's grant was transferred from BR to the PTE, and reduced by 10% each year, the difference being raised through a corresponding annually increased percept on the domestic rates levied by the West Midlands County Council. This arrangement brought greater co-ordination of train and bus services; and joint bus and rail prepaid TravelCard tickets, which offered maximum flexibility in the use of public transport.

In anticipation of bus deregulation on 4 October 1986, WMPTE's rail services began to be promoted under the Midline banner; WMPTE's bus services being operated by a new private company, West Midlands Travel, from later in that month. From May 1987 Wolverhampton's Stour Valley EMU local services were extended to run through New Street to Walsall, and morning and evening rush hour trains began to run through to Birmingham International and Coventry. The basic weekday pattern over the

line now sees 16 trains leaving Wolverhampton, eight of which have worked through from Stafford. The Stour Valley line has also been improved through funds made available from the West Midlands County Council's Greenline project. Six former industrial sites between Wolverhampton and Birmingham were landscaped under a £162,000 facelift programme, and 12 life-size steel horses, designed by artist Keith Atherton, were unveiled on 13 March 1987 by the running of a special train.

Under the enthusiastic support of the PTE, the West Midlands has enjoyed an unforeseen increase in local rail commuter traffic in recent years. The successful promotion of Park-and-Ride facilities, notably at Stourbridge Junction, has led to the reopening of certain lines, such as that between Walsall and Hednesford, and to the development of proposals to build additional stations along the Stour Valley line. Much of this depends upon the completion of a second cross-city line by the reinstatement of the line between Smethwick West and the newly rebuilt Snow Hill station, which will release service capacity on the Stour Valley line between Galton Junction and New Street by the diversion of some Stourbridge services to Snow Hill. If this goes ahead, the first new station will be at Spring Vale, adjacent to the site of the former Bilston steelworks and just beyond the site of the former Ettingshall Road and Bilston station. Further planned stations include: St Vincent Street, currently under construction by the site of the former Monument Lane shed to serve Birmingham's new convention centre; Galton Bridge, just beyond Galton Junction and near to the site of the former Spon Lane station; and a station just to the north of Bushbury Junction, as yet unnamed, to serve expanded residential developments in the Bushbury and Oxley areas and to offer Park-and-Ride facilities to users of the M54 and proposed Western Orbital Route.

2 — InterCity passenger services

Wolverhampton High Level's twilight existence during its years of redevelopment gave little indication of the activity it was to enjoy in more recent years. Starved of Euston services, the few that remained were rescheduled to start from Birmingham New Street from 8 September 1963, working ecs from the High Level carriage sheds via the station's goods avoiding lines. Steam was also ousted as electrification work proceeded, with express steam locomotives being banned on BR (LMR) lines south of Crewe from 1 September 1964, followed by a ban on all steam through workings between Crewe and Euston, which was originally scheduled for 1 January 1965 but postponed until that September due to a lack of diesel replacements.

As a result of this, Bushbury shed's allocation of steam locomotives had declined to such an extent that it became uneconomical to keep it open, so it closed on 12 April 1965, its remaining allocation being transferred to Oxley; the 14-acre site being sold on 28 August 1970. The Stafford Road works site was also sold, the main buildings being demolished in April 1969 but the former engine sheds survived until they were found to be unsafe, and they were knocked down from 9 February 1978.

By late 1965 electrification work had progressed so far that the regular electric locomotive haulage of main line passenger trains from Euston could begin on 22 November 1965, all movements into and out of the station becoming by electric traction from 3 January 1966. The new LMR timetable, commencing on 18 April 1966, also contained good news for Wolverhampton rail users with the reinstatement of two evening fast through services to Euston, which were to be electric-hauled south of Coventry; and the diversion of the down 'Emerald Isle Express' via Birmingham and Wolverhampton to provide the town with a direct Holyhead boat connection. The electric working of main line trains was also further extended to Birmingham New Street from 5 December 1966.

Full electric working from Wolverhampton High Level began on 6 March 1967, and was based upon a

Left:
Since electrification, Wolverhampton's local services have been maintained by a mixture of DMUs, Sprinters and EMUs. This is how they looked back in April 1967, from the passenger footway. *Brian Haresnape*

Below:
Oxley shed seen on its penultimate day, 2 March 1967, with a pair of Stanier Black 5s. *Mike Wood*

Bottom:
The 'new' erecting shop at Stafford Road works topples to the ground in April 1969. *Ned Williams*

strict 15min past the hour departure from Euston between 08.15 and 20.15, with additional trains at 17.50 and 22.15; these and the 20.15 Euston departure all terminating at Wolverhampton. The 08.15 from Birmingham, and the 18.15 down from Euston, also contained a Shrewsbury portion, then the only through London to Shrewsbury service. All of the remaining services continued alternately to Liverpool or Manchester, with an 11min wait at Birmingham New Street. The first three morning services started at Wolverhampton, with the remainder commencing either at Liverpool or Manchester, the 'Birmingham Pullman's' mantle being assumed by a short-lived morning service styled 'The Executive', which required the compulsory reservation of dining seats at a 7s 6d first-class and 5s second-class surcharge. Completing the changes brought about on 6 March 1967 was the

diversion of the 'West Coast Postal' mail train from the Trent Valley line to run via the Stour Valley line, with a pickup stop at Wolverhampton. Finally, from mid-June to the start of September 1967 a daily through train ran between Wolverhampton and Aberystwyth. With slight changes to their timings, this was the basic pattern of InterCity services serving Wolverhampton for the next five years.

From 1 May 1972 major improvements were introduced in the frequency of services on the routes linking London with Birmingham and Bristol. Birmingham New Street became the focus of a revision of cross-country services linking North and Southwest England and South Wales. A new half-hourly service was introduced between London and Birmingham, with Euston-New Street timings of

Above:
The remains of Stafford Road Nos 1, 2 & 3 sheds await demolition on 9 February 1978. *Ned Williams Collection*

Below:
An IC125 unit passes Wolverhampton North Junction. These began running to Liverpool and Manchester via Wolverhampton in May 1984. The North Junction was reinstated in August 1966 to allow trains from the High Level station to once more take the ex-S&B line to Shrewsbury. *Ned Williams*

90-95min and trains leaving Euston at 10min and 40min past the hour; the former all travelling at least as far as Wolverhampton, the latter all

Above:
Amongst the more interesting of the cross-country trains serving Wolverhampton is the 09.50 Paignton-Glasgow service which usually changes to electric traction there. On 18 July 1986 No 50041 *Bulwark* is seen, Wolverhampton-bound, crossing the canal at Albion. *John Whitehouse*

terminating at Birmingham. As a result of this, many more London trains also began at Wolverhampton, requiring the changes at Oxley already described.

On 6 May 1974 the culmination of a four-year £75 million resignalling and electrification project saw the introduction of all-electric train services between Euston and Glasgow. The work had involved the electrification and resignalling of the West Coast main line between Weaver Junction, north of Crewe, and Motherwell, south of Glasgow; plus the construction of new electric locomotives, the Class 87s. From Birmingham, and hence through Wolverhampton, to Glasgow and Edinburgh, the previous daily service of one train per day was increased to four per day in each direction, one also being extended south to begin and terminate at Bristol.

About an hour was taken off the journey time from Wolverhampton to Glasgow or Edinburgh, which could now be reached in 4hr. An additional service, styled 'The Clansman', left Euston at 09.35 and arrived at Inverness at 19.45 calling at Wolverhampton; an up 'Clansman' leaving Inverness at 10.30 and arriving at Euston at 21.04. Also, from the summer of 1974, BR's latest Mk 3 coaching stock was introduced on the Anglo-Scottish electric services, the 75ft 5in vehicles being capable of sustained speeds up to a maximum of 125mph.

These services are maintained and augmented daily Manchester and Liverpool IC125 workings began in May 1984 and through workings to Exeter, Plymouth and Penzance have been instated. On 14 December 1987 the 09.26 Euston train was the first push-pull set worked West Coast lines public service (with a Class 86 locomotive and ex-IC125 power car 43 123), and Class 90 locomotives with Driving Van Trailers now regularly work Euston services. On 14 December 1989 BR declared Wolverhampton one of only five centres from which daytime Channel Tunnel services to Paris and Brussels would originate. From 1 June 1993, twice daily morning Trent and Stour Valley line trains from Manchester and Wolverhampton will be joined at Rugby and run non-stop to Europe.

3 — Freight facilities and services

Wolverhampton's main freight facilities have also undergone great changes in the last 25 years. In March 1964 BR announced a plan for a series of steel concentration yards in the West Midlands, with existing goods yards at Great Bridge and Wolverhampton to be developed to provide railheads for the receipt and delivery of steel for the Black Country. Accordingly, the ex-OWW Walsall Street Goods Depot was closed and demolished in late 1965, the site being remodelled and reopened as a steel terminal under the name of Wolverhampton New Depot on 31 May 1966.

Whilst all this remodelling work was being done, Wolverhampton was also the origin of the heaviest single load then ever to be carried on British Railways when three 240-ton boilers manufactured by John Thompson Ltd, each 122ft long by 26ft 6in in circumference, were moved from Ettingshall Road to the site of a new CEGB power station at Eggborough near Goole in Yorkshire.

Central to BR's freight operations in the West Midlands was to be a remodelled Bescot yard, which came into full operation on 18 April 1966, with all northbound freight movements being electric-hauled. Bescot acted as a central freight concentration point and allowed other more dispersed yards to be dispensed with; accordingly Bushbury sidings were closed a few weeks beforehand. Later

Left:
Gloucester-built Class 128 Motor Parcels Van No W55995 proves that the class could haul a tail-load as it takes the ex-OWW line out of Wolverhampton Low Level in the early 1960s. *J. B. Bucknall*

Centre left:
Wolverhampton steel terminal was constructed on the site of the former OWW Walsall Street Goods and opened on 31 May 1966. Currently undergoing an increase in traffic, the terminal, which also controls those at Wednesbury and Brierley Hill, is seen here on 16 August 1988 as a Class 47-hauled InterCity train passes on the Stour Valley line en route to Wolverhampton. *Author*

Below left:
Monmore Green basin was built by the Chillington Iron Works but taken over by the LNWR in the 1890s. As shown here it now serves as a siding for the adjacent steel terminal and was photographed on 16 August 1988 as an InterCity train passed en route to Wolverhampton station. *Guy Sunbeam*

Below:
Delapidated but still open, Wednesfield Road goods station now serves as part of Wolverhampton steel terminal, although it carries the marks of its former glory. *Keith Hodgkins*

that year, on 15 August, the overhead on the whole of the Stafford-Coventry-Rugby section of the Grand Junction line was energised, also allowing southbound freight workings from Bescot.

The ex-GWR Herbert Street Goods Depot was operated by National Carriers Ltd from 1967, but closed on 27 March 1972, since when the buildings, still in a remarkable state of repair, have belonged to a builders merchant; but all rail connections to the depot were not finally severed until February 1982. Monmore Green basin remains open, but only as additional sidings for the steel terminal. It was joined on 24 September 1971 by a new branch to an adjacent depot opened by British Oxygen. Wednesfield Road Goods was leased to Railstores Ltd, but they had made little use of the buildings for many months before the lease expired in October 1988, although the yard is still used by BR as another offshoot of Wolverhampton steel terminal, which has seen a remarkable growth of traffic in recent years. The BR steel terminals at Wednesbury and Brierley Hill are also controlled from Wolverhampton, which makes all collection, storage and delivery arrangements. Recent operational changes at all three terminals have been aimed at eliminating steel movements through Bescot to free its capacity for Speedlink services. Accordingly, Wednesbury now receives its steel traffic from Cardiff; Brierley Hill's comes from Scunthorpe, and Wolverhampton's from Lackenby, near Redcar.

There are five basic daily services supplying the three steel terminals: two from Cardiff, which call at Brierley Hill en route to Wednesbury; two from Scunthorpe, which call at Wolverhampton, Wednesbury and Brierley Hill, and one from Lackenby direct to Wolverhampton. Each day the three terminals

handle about 5,000 tons of steel, 4,000 tons of which passes through the same day, and 1,000 tons of which is stored; the latter wagons being sent to Wednesfield Road to be unloaded. In 1986-87, 580,000 tons of steel was handled in this way, and in 1987-88 this figure had increased to 672,000 tons.

Saddest of all amongst Wolverhampton's goods buildings had been the old High Level station carriage drive entrance building, the former offices of the Wolverhampton District Goods Manager. Since being vacated by the resignalling engineers in early 1971, these had stood empty, a home to vandals and vagrants. By 1975 they were unsafe and faced demolition, but were rescued by a concerned council and County Council. They were listed Grade II on 3 February 1977, and the unsound wings fronting Railway Street and Horseley Fields were demolished at the end of July 1979. Shored up, the remaining central arched portion stood for a further nine years, until work began on 17 May 1988 to convert it into an enquiries bureau for West Midlands Travel.

Below left:
The former Wolverhampton DGMO stood empty for eight years; a home to vandals and vagrants, before the buildings to either side were demolished in July 1979; a month after this photograph was taken.
Wolverhampton Library

Bottom:
Work on restoring the former High Level station carriage entrance drive building, listed Grade II on 3 February 1977, began on 17 May 1988. This was the progress made by 10 June 1988. *Author*

Right:
From 6 May 1974 a new Euston-Inverness service, styled 'The Clansman' was introduced. Here No 86228 *Vulcan Heritage* arrives at Wolverhampton with the down Clansman on a snowy 19 January 1985. *Chris Morrison*

Below right:
Excursions sometimes still bring unusual motive power to Wolverhampton such as on this occasion when No 46007 brought a five-coach SAGA Holidays extra through the station. *Clive Jarrad*

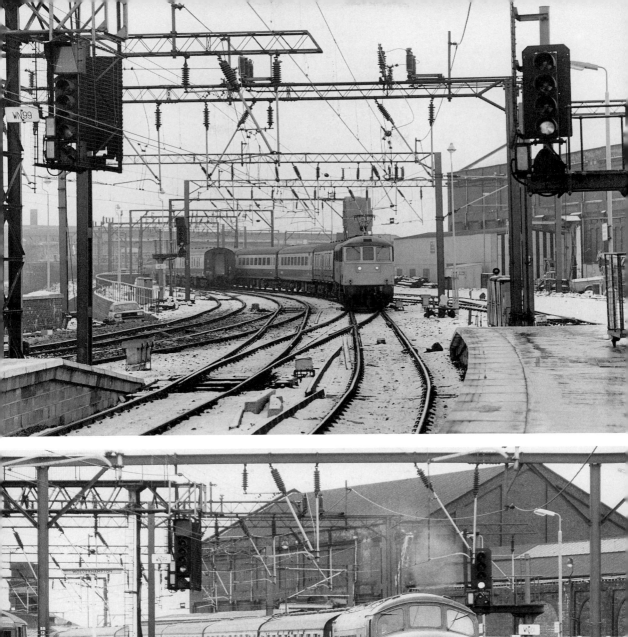

6: Proposed Lines and Miscellaneous Railway Activity

Proposed Lines

As complicated as Wolverhampton's railways became, they were as nothing compared to the situation that would have existed if all of the lines proposed to connect with the town had been built. That said, two of the earliest proposals took routes similar to ones adopted by lines that were eventually constructed. The Birmingham, Dudley, Stourbridge and Wolverhampton scheme was to be engineered by George Leather and was promoted in 1837, the line to run from the centre of Birmingham, via Soho, Winson Green, West Bromwich, Burnt Tree (near Dudley), Coseley and Ettingshall, to Wolverhampton, with a branch to Stourbridge from Tipton via Dudley. Powers to build this line were obtained but not exercised, although the route was later used, in part, by the GWR's BW&D.

Similarly, the Grand Connection Railway, to be engineered by George Landmann, was also promoted in 1837; obtained its powers, but was not built. This was to have run from a junction with the Birmingham & Gloucester line at Wadborough near Pershore, via Norton, Worcester, Fernall Heath, Kidderminster, Wall Heath, Swindon, The Bratch (Wombourn), Finchfield and Chapel Ash, to a two-way junction with the GJR line at Wolverhampton. Ten years later, the OWW company adopted a nearly identical route between Pershore and Kidderminster, and was able to make use of the extensive traffic surveys undertaken by the Grand Connection's promoters; and part of the line's course through Wombourn was later used by the GWR's B&W line.

In 1845, at the height of the railway mania, four proposed lines had Wolverhampton connections. Three: the Wolverhampton Bridgnorth & Ludlow; the Wolverhampton Chester & Birkenhead Junction, and the Wolverhampton Walsall & Atherstone, were purely speculative; but the fourth, the London Worcester & South Staffordshire, was more malicious in its intent; being promoted jointly by the L&B and Midland companies in an attempt to block the GWR-supported O&R and OWW Bills then before Parliament. None received approval.

Things quietened down after the mania, and Wolverhampton did not feature again in a railway proposal until 1865, when the Bridgnorth Wolverhampton & Staffordshire Railway was promoted to connect the Severn Valley line, from a junction at Oldbury (Shropshire), to the GWR at Wolverhampton. Powers were obtained for this on 28 June 1866, but it too was not constructed.

Most of the proposed lines mentioned so far existed more in the minds of their promoters than the public. The same cannot be said of the Midland Birmingham Wolverhampton & Milford Junction Railway (MBW&MJR), proposed by the Midland company in 1882. Engineered by John Addison, this 37-mile line commenced at a junction with the Shrewsbury & Hereford Railway just south of Craven Arms & Stokesay station, and proceeded northeast through Brockhampton, Morville, Bridgnorth, Claverley, Bobbington, Wombourn and Sedgley, to Wolverhampton High Level; proceeding to a junction with the Midland's W&W line just west of Willenhall (Market Place) station. In addition, four branches would give the line connections with the Stour Valley and Grand Junction lines, the Bishop's Castle Railway and the Central Wales Railway, which, with the addition of running powers over 12 companies' lines, would enable it to fulfil the 'Milford Junction' part of its name.

Support for the MBW&MJR was forthcoming from, amongst others, Wolverhampton Town Council. Opposition was also aroused in many of the towns and villages along its route, most notably in Bishop's Castle and Penn, where, at the latter the railway was planned to divide the local common. A costly diversion was forced here by solicitors acting for the Commons Preservation Society; and the line became similarly bogged down in legal actions brought by other local and national groups. Although the MBW&MJR was rejected by the House of Lords in 1883, most of its proposals (minus the Bishop's Castle link) received the Royal Assent in 1884 under the simpler name of the Midland & Central Wales Junction Railway. But the following year a Bill was placed before Parliament to abandon these powers, the Midland having found that it could reach the places the line was intended to connect much more cheaply by obtaining running powers over existing lines.

The 20th century has seen two light railways proposed for Wolverhampton. The Wolverhampton & Cannock Chase Railway was promoted at the height of the light railway boom in 1900; obtaining powers on 17 August 1901 for a 8¾-mile standard gauge line, from a junction with the GWR's Cannock

An artist's impression of one of the Light Rapid Transit vehicles intended to be used on the proposed Midland Metro lines. Part railway, part street tramway, the first line is scheduled to be built between Birmingham and Wolverhampton, utilising, for the most part, the trackbed of the former GWR BW&D line. It may be commenced as early as 1991. *Midland Metro/WMPTE*

Road Junction-Bushbury Junction line to a junction with the LNWR's Walsall to Cannock line at Cannock, to be worked either by steam or electric traction. Construction was delayed, and Extension of Time Acts were obtained in 1905, 1907 and 1910, the last lapsing in 1913, when the whole scheme was vested in the LNWR. Nothing more was heard of it until 1920, when it was revived by the latter that December in an application to the Light Railway Commissioners. Now to connect with LNWR lines at both ends, and shortened to 6½ miles, permission to build the line was obtained, but somehow it was overlooked in the run-up to the Grouping, and the LMS did not proceed with it.

Hopefully a better fate awaits the light railways contained in the Midland Metro proposals announced on 27 August 1987. Inspired by the success of the Tyne & Wear Metro, this is one of a number of Light Rapid Transit or 'Supertram' schemes currently being promoted in the country which is intended to utilise both street tramways and adapted British Rail lines. Whilst covering the whole West Midlands, a line between Birmingham and Wolverhampton is scheduled to be the first built. Utilising most of the trackbed of the GWR's BW&D line as far as Stow Heath, this will then travel along the Bilston Road into Wolverhampton town centre. A Bill to authorise this line is to be presented before Parliament in November 1988, and the line expected to be in operation by 1993.

Railway Contractors

Wolverhampton also became the home of several railway contractors, who supplied their products and expertise to railways both home and abroad.

Henry Lovatt & Co

Henry Lovatt began as an architect in practice in Wolverhampton from the early 1850s. In 1858, like many other provincial architects of the period, Lovatt also began to undertake building work, hiring labourers and craftsmen and overseeing construction personally. He enjoyed great success, and soon began to take on work for the major railway companies, notably the GWR and, later, the Great Central. A fair representation of the railway contracts his company worked on can be gained from a look at the work it undertook in the early years of this century. This included Oxley locomotive shed (GWR, 1906-07), the Tickhill Light

Railway (Great Northern Railway, 1910-11), station buildings, Birmingham Snow Hill (GWR, 1910), widening and reconstruction at Rochester (SE&CR, 1910), reconstruction of King's Cross station (Metropolitan Railway, 1911), and the Ealing & Shepherds Bush Railway (GWR, 1914).

In 1915, the firm became known as Wilson Lovatt & Co and went public under this name in 1952, splitting to form the Wilson Lovatt Group, based in Wolverhampton, London and Norwich, on 1 January 1965. Railway contracting continued; that year the firm built a (diesel-electric) locomotive depot for BR (LMR) at Bletchley, and reconstructed depots at Swindon, and at Temple Mills in London. Further expansion occurred in the group, which over-reached itself, having to call in a receiver in February 1971, and folding, with the loss of 400 jobs in the Midlands alone.

ABC Coupler Ltd

The Automatic Buffing Contact (ABC) Coupler and Engineering Company was incorporated on 3 March 1904, and was at first an agency, subcontracting work to outside manufacturers and having products made under licence. It became established at a works in Fallings Park Wolverhampton in 1915, which was also the company's registered office from 1939. Though manufacturers of all types of railway coupling devices — the typical British hook and shackle, three-link chain; 'Instanter' link, and screw shackle kinds — the company was best known for variants on couplers using the ABC principle. In this, buffers and couplers are one unit, which uses a shackle in conjunction with a revolving vertical hook that engages automatically on impact with another

similarly equipped railway vehicle. These were well suited for use on narrow gauge lines, and the company built up an extensive export trade.

A wholly-owned subsidiary company, Wota Ltd, produced other railway components such as axle-boxes, bearings, regulator valves and bypass valves, some of which were manufactured under licence. Heavily inhibited by trade restrictions during World War 2 the firm flourished in the postwar period with increased demand from railways undergoing reconstruction. Towards the end of the 1950s, the company was engaged in the manufacture, design and sale of ABC-style couplers, regulator valves, handling equipment and industrial lubricants, and began the development of new products, most notably of a wagon side buffer.

Sadly, over half a century's expertise in railway engineering was undermined by behind-the-scenes share dealings that only succeeded in weakening the company's financial position and ended in it being formally wound up on 7 June 1962. Its assets and patents were acquired by the Wednesbury firm of F. H. Lloyd & Co later in 1962. The Fallings Park works was closed, but coupler production continued as the ABC Coupler Division of Lloyd's, until it too closed in 1984.

E. C. & J. Keay Ltd

The James Bridge works of F. H. Lloyd & Co was an appropriate place for the manufacture of railway components as it adjoined the works of E. C. & J. Keay, railway signal engineers. Keay was probably one of this country's oldest structural engineering companies, being established in West Bromwich in 1879. Expansion required the move to the larger

James Bridge site in 1887, and by the turn of the century the company had also begun to produce railway signalling equipment, including signal cabins and interlocking lever frames. Like Wilson Lovatt & Co, Keays worked extensively for the GWR, and were particularly noted for making and installing steel railway bridges, listing the fabrication and erection of every railway bridge between Birmingham and Stratford-on-Avon with pride amongst its publicity as late as the 1970s! Structural work for the GWR also included the steelwork for

both Birmingham Snow Hill and Paddington stations, plus the Great Western Royal Hotel at Paddington. After World War 2 the company diversified away from the production of signalling equipment towards more general structural engineering, and, like ABC Coupler, ended its days as part of the F. H. Lloyd Group.

Henry Meadows Ltd

Henry Meadows Ltd was formed in 1920 to manufacture and supply three-speed gearboxes to the country's then large number of independent car makers, and, like ABC Coupler Ltd, was based at Fallings Park in Wolverhampton. In 1922 the firm also began to produce petrol engines, which, over the years, were used to power such famous marques as Bean, Fraser-Nash, Lea-Francis, Invicta and Lagonda. Just before World War 2 the company began to experiment with diesel engines, and in 1947 produced a range of square bore/stroke ratio units for a variety of transport applications. Joint work with the firm of D. Wickham & Co Ltd of Ware brought Meadows engines into diesel rail traction; one of its collaborations being on the two double-bogie railcars Wickham supplied to the Bas Congo Katanga Railway in July 1954, each of which was powered by one Meadows 130bhp engine. But it is a later Wickham collaboration, on five of the 22

Left:
Henry Lovatt & Co undertook a great deal of civil engineering work for railway companies, and so had its own stock of railway wagons, some of which are seen behind GWR 'Sir Daniel' class No 478. This engine spent most of its time in the Bristol area, which is therefore a likely location for the photograph. *LPC*

Below:
In addition to its obvious products, the ABC Coupler Co also produced other railway components such as axleboxes, bearings, bypass valves, and, as shown here, regulators. Their greatest market was overseas, amongst the many narrow gauge lines built in former British colonies. *Triplex-Lloyd*

railbuses ordered by BR in May 1957 (SC 79965-69) that is better known. These were powered by a Meadows 6HDT500, six-cylinder, 8.14-litre flat diesel engine, and were used on branch lines in the Scottish Region during the late 1950s and early 1960s.

Above:
The five railbuses (SC 79965-79969) built for BR in 1958 were powered by six HDT 500, six-cylinder, 8.14-litre flat diesel engines manufactured by Henry Meadows Ltd of Wolverhampton. Here, SC 79965, the first completed, is seen emerging from its maker's shops at Ware in October 1958. *Ian Allan Library*

Industrial Lines in the Wolverhampton Area

A number of the large firms in the Wolverhampton area had their own internal railway systems. These included The Patent Shaft & Axletree Co at Wednesbury, Stewarts & Lloyd's (later British Steel) steelworks at Bilston (which had both standard gauge lines and a 2ft gauge system to carry steel ingots around the works), and the Wolverhampton Gas Co. Also of interest to this story was the once extensive system operated by Courtaulds Ltd at its Dunstall Hill works, which was built from 1924 onwards, and was opened fully in 1926. This plant came to specialise in the production of viscous rayon yarns, and was doubled in size during 1937 by the addition of a warp-knitting mill to produce knitted rayon fabrics, all of which required daily movements of coal and chemicals into the works.

Courtaulds employed two Hawthorn Leslie 0-4-0 inside-cylinder saddle tanks, of 1927 and 1936 vintage for most of their shunting movements, except on a celebrated occasion in December 1957 when one of these was away for repair. The company hired a replacement 0-4-0 locomotive from BR which supplied L&Y 'Pug' saddle tank No 51204, the only one of its class ever to work in the Wolverhampton area. The sidings and lines at Courtaulds were accessed via a ¼-mile connection with the former GWR B&W Wombourn line near Oxley. With the closure of this line looming on 1 March 1965, the company changed to road transport in late 1964, but closed in 1971, the last remains of its railway system being removed by January 1973.

The British Oxygen depot branch (noted in Chapter 5) is the only industrial line remaining in use in Wolverhampton, although, until recently, the line serving the former British Steel works near Horseley Fields, which connected with British Rail on the ex-W&W line at Heath Town Junction, was in operation.

Appendices

Appendix 1
LNWR — Statement of number of trains in, out and through Wolverhampton (High Level) station daily, March 1877

8am-8pm No	8pm-8am No		In	Out	Through	Total
80	27	Passenger trains	36	36	35	107
20	16	Goods trains	11	10	15	36
3	1	Mineral trains	—	—	4	4
14	9	Light engines	11	12	—	23
		Total number of trains daily				170

LNWR — Statement showing the number of passengers and weight of merchandise traffic into and out of Wolverhampton (High Level) station for the year 1876

Particulars	No of passengers	Goods (tons)	Minerals (tons)	Total goods & minerals
Traffic to and from places north of Wolverhampton	195,073	79,869	35,911	115,780
Traffic to and from places south of Wolverhampton	740,953	79,951	17,860	97,811
Total	936,026	159,820	53,771	213,591

Appendix 2
OWW — Return of rolling stock delivered up to 10 August 1855

Engines delivered by C. C. Williams

12 passenger engines by Hawthorn, 16in cylinders, 5ft 9in wheels, 4-coupled

8 goods engines by Hawthorn, 17in cylinders, 5ft wheels, 6-coupled

6 passenger engines by Wilson, 16in cylinders, 5ft 9in wheels, 4-coupled

Engines purchased by the OWW from E. B. Wilson & Co, Leeds

1 'Jenny Lind' 14in cylinders, 5ft 6in driving wheels

2 tank engines, 9in cylinders, 5ft 6in wheels, 4-coupled, leading and driving wheels 3ft 6in diameter, trailing wheels 3ft

4 goods engines, 16in cylinders, 5ft wheels, 6-coupled

2 goods engines, 16in cylinders, 4ft 9in wheels, 6-coupled

2 passenger engines, 15in cylinders, leading wheels 4ft, driving and trailing wheels 6ft 6in, 4-coupled

By Sharp Stewart

1 goods engine, 18in cylinders, 5ft wheels, 6-coupled

By R. Stephenson & Co

2 goods engines, 18in cylinders, 5ft wheels, 6-coupled

Ordered from E. B. Wilson

4 tank engines, 15in cylinders, leading and driving wheels 4ft 6in, coupled trailing wheels 3ft 6in

4 express engines, 15in cylinders, 6ft 3in driving wheels

5 goods engines, 16in cylinders, 5ft wheels, 6-coupled

Stephenson & Co

5 goods engines, 17½in cylinders, 5ft wheels, 6-coupled

2 passenger engines, 15in cylinders, 6ft 6in driving wheels

Carriage and wagon stock

22 first class
15 composites
35 second class
59 third class
20 luggage brake vans
10 horse boxes
9 carriage trucks
20 goods brake vans
4 10-ton brake vans
17 cattle wagons
6 coke wagons
228 high-sided wagons
234 coal wagons
60 low-sided wagons
50 Hensons covered wagons
12 timber trucks

Appendix 3
GWR Chief Mechanical Engineer's Department divisional expenses and statistics. Wolverhampton Division Sheds. Four weeks ending 26 June 1937 (27 June 1936)

Total locomotive stock	611	(624)
Locomotives in use	473	(476)
Locomotives not used	10	(10)
Locomotives awaiting repair	29	(37)
Locomotives awaiting repair at other depots in Division	5	(4)
Locomotives awaiting Swindon attention	30	(24)
Locomotives awaiting boiler examinations, etc	16	(16)

Locomotives in Stafford Road works	48	(57)
Maximum number of locomotives in use on any one weekday	476	(481)
Average daily engine miles	115	(112)
Daily engine hours per locomotive in traffic (144hr week)	12.8	(12.31)
Total regular locomotive mileage (passenger)	581,782	(579,025)
Total special locomotive mileage (passenger)	60,780	(82,306)
Mileage of diesel cars	7,527	(7,865)
Total registered locomotive mileage (freight)	718,643	(657,118)
Total locomotive hours (passenger)	50,886	(52,044)
Total locomotive hours (freight)	100,458	(90,603)
Total hours diesel cars	819	(981)
Coal consumption (tons)	29,503	(28,772)
No of weeks' stock	2	(2)
Pounds of coal consumed per engine/mile (passenger)	45.64	
Pounds of coal consumed per engine/mile (freight)	47.80	
Gallons of diesel consumed by diesel cars	897	
Pints of locomotive lubricating oil consumed (passenger)	44,980	
Pints of locomotive lubricating oil consumed (freight)	47,450	
Pints of locomotive lubricating oil consumed (diesel cars)	315	
Enginemen	1,055	(1,022)
Firemen	1,039	(1,001)
Boiler Washers	51	(51)
Engine Cleaners	225	(243)
Shedmen	326	(331)
Coalmen	53	(53)
Hydraulic Enginemen	7	(7)
Water Pumping Enginemen	10	(14)
Hydraulic & Steam Cranemen	5	(5)
Gas Makers & Assistants	6	(6)
Carriage & Wagon Examiners	154	(155)
Carriage Cleaners/Washers and Bogie Oilers (male)	222	(219)
Carriage Cleaners/Washers and Bogie Oilers (female)	3	(3)
Carriage & Wagon Greasers and Oilers	67	(64)
Oil Gas Fillers & Lighting staff	3	(3)
Fitters	105	(105)
Blacksmiths	26	(26)
Mechanics	28	(28)
Labourers	145	(145)
Carriage & Wagon Mechanics	62	(63)
Carriage & Wagon Labourers	41	(43)
Miscellaneous	1	(1)
Foremen & Inspectors	11	(12)
Clerks (male)	49	(50)
Clerks (female)	10	(10)

Salaried staff

Foremen and Inspectors	42	(42)
Running Shed Clerks	15	(15)
Divisional Officers	43	(43)
Average wages (Enginemen)	98s 9d	(95s 11d)
Average wages (Firemen)	75s 11d	(77s 0d)

Stafford Road locomotive works

Total number of employees	436	(433)
Total salaries and wages paid	£6,722	(£5,765)
Cost of work done	£1,119	(£994)
Total in year to date	£38,197	(£38,410)

Appendix 4
Locomotives in Stafford Road Locomotive Works 1938

21/01	19/02	21/03	20/04	20/05	21/06	14/07	19/08	21/09	21/10	23/11	20/12
1808	2084	1527	1527	1763	1773	1773	1787	1788	2155	892	1783
1810	2129	1779	1749	2071	2030	1787	2146	2028	2536	1783	2055
2274	2385	1965	1763	2156	2071	2030	2320	2078	2572	2092	2102
2389	2452	2084	1965	2257	2401	2258	2345	2320	2772	2152	2152
2711	2460	2256	2256	2425	2425	2464	2348	2345	2777	2155	2262
2719	2523	2270	2257	2462	2464	2488	2538	2348	2778	2256	2281
3450	2741	2385	2569	2490	3276	2716	2716	2538	3284	2262	2287
3561	3205	2392	3150	3150	3574	2791	2717	2665	4107	2660	2753
4053	3450	2452	3203	3575	4596	3276	2745	3563	4386	3210	2758
4838	3562	2523	3575	5103	5102	3574	2791	4110	4546	4400	2924
5135	4401	2569	4501	5105	5139	4856	3563	4111	4575	4403	3445
5152	4812	2706	4801	5106	5144	5102	3574	4386	5109	5109	4400
5154	4864	2741	5103	5139	5153	5125	4111	4546	5128	5119	4403
5192	5084	3450	5106	5143	5163	5127	5125	4811	5171	5128	5119
5723	5116	4140	5143	5160	5164	5165	5147	5125	5174	5131	5127
5743	5135	4501	5155	5164	5166	5185	5150	5184	5188	5135	5131
6338	5138	4816	5175	5168	5179	5345	5162	5186	5317	5167	5147
6341	5143	5130	5189	5181	5185	5370	5165	5317	5667	5188	5153
6405	5153	5155	5312	5193	5193	6378	5345	5404	5673	5323	5156
7318	5166	5180	5324	6380	5370	6602	6369	5738	5791	5394	5175
7320	5181	6334	5727	8787	6380	6624	6376	5794	5794	5667	5179
7705	5192	6349	6348	9742	6602	7319	2287*	5811	7315	5810	5196
7750	5957	6684	6349	9768	9715	8309	2475*	6698	8322	6001	5199
8332	6327	7310	6361	2488*	9742	9715	2572*	8798	9774	6335	5323
8334	6341	7758	6403	5163*	9768	2146*	2665*	2092*	9782	6389	5541
8344	7234	8333	7237	5179*	2258*	2745*	4546*	2287*	892*	6418	5807
8393	7310	6315*	7702	5185*	2791*	4103*	4930*	2772*	2092*	7420	5810
9719	7750	6403*	7758	6602*	3208*	5147*	5184*	2777*	2152*	8322	9728
9727	8334	9714*	9714	9752*	3574*	5150*	5186*	2778*	3020*	9728	2536*
9730	9719	9769*	9769		4103*	5162*	5187*	3016*	3210*	9782	6342*
2579*	2451*	3203†	1779*		4702*		5811*	3043*	4013*	2536*	6335†
3273*	2706*	3414†	2383*		4856*		6698*	3579*	4403*	3445*	
1488‡	6307*		2462*		5127*		8798*	4107*	5810*	4337*	
	8332*		3016*		5150*			4575*	6744*	4704*	
	8339†		5160*		5165*			5061*	8390*	5147*	
			5193*		5345*			5144*	5144†	5153*	
			7236*		5754*			5171*		7706*	
			6601†		6378*			5188*			
					6624*			5791*			
					7319*			9748*			
								9774*			
								9782*			
								4873†			

* Locomotive in the yard awaiting repair.
† Locomotive on the weighbridge.
‡ Locomotive broken up.